Don't Do Anything I Would~~n't~~ Do

Don't Do Anything I Would Do

Essays on Dating, Divorce, and Romantic Delusions

CARA ALWILL

CHAMPAGNE PROBLEMS PRESS

To all the girls who wear their heart on their sleeve:

You will laugh again. You will feel beautiful again.
You will fall in love again. You will have hope again.
You will feel empowered again. You will feel good again.
You will be yourself again. Maybe even better.

XOXO
Cara

CONTENTS

You Haven't Been Yourself in a Long Time — 1

Miami Heat — 13

You've Got Male — 23

My Bumble Profile — 33

The Jukebox is Broken — 37

Why Are My Lips Numb? — 45

Spellbound — 51

Paris Syndrome — 63

My Very Beautiful Friend — 75

To Live and Date in LA — 83

Love Letters — 91

Happy New Year — 97

Love Lessons — 101

The Space Between — 113

A Change of Heart — 119

The Last Goodbye? — 127

PREFACE

YOU HAVEN'T BEEN
YOURSELF IN A LONG TIME

You haven't been yourself in a long time, a friend said to me
a few years into my post-divorce dating life.

First, her words pissed me off. Who the hell was she to tell
me who I was or wasn't?

Next, I was in denial. *That's not true*, I thought. *I'm totally
myself. I'm completely fine! Happy even!* (as I sat there staring at
the guy's Instagram story I was sort of dating even though he
refused to call it dating, trying to determine whether or not he
was sleeping with the girl he just posted).

Then, I was sad. Because I knew she was right. I had not
been myself at all since my divorce.

I was lost. Completely unrecognizable to those closest to
me. The confident, optimistic, level-headed version of me was
dead. Suddenly an insecure, fearful, *chaotic* version of me had

1

taken over her role in the movie of my life. And it wasn't cute.

I knew I was lost at the time, but I didn't think anyone else knew it. Even after the intervention-style phone calls, even after the "Nobody understands what you see in him!" and the "I pray for you daily that you'll wake up" texts—no, I'm not being dramatic either. My friends were fucking praying for me. I mean, it's so kind, but it's also kind of alarming.

Before we go on, you should know that I am a smart, successful woman. I run my own business. I am financially independent. I have a high IQ and a high credit score. I have always been a positive, well-adjusted person who makes good choices (except maybe when ordering a late night delivery of Flaming Hot Cheetos from my local 711 after drinking a bottle of wine—but let's not go there right now). I generally have my shit together.

I was a bit of a late bloomer in the romance department. As a kid and through my teens especially, I was always self-conscious about my weight and this made me insecure around guys. I was never fat, but I wasn't thin either. And as a child growing up in the nineties, THIN was in and it was a goal I never reached (gorgeous babes like Ashley Graham who have now made curves cool had not yet entered the chat). As a result, my self-esteem was in the gutter and I spent most of my formative years developing massive crushes on guys who didn't even know I existed, or at least that's how I felt.

I was not the girl with a high school sweetheart. I never had a great teenage love story I could look back on fondly years later. I didn't have a college boyfriend who I wistfully parted ways with after graduation that I could Facebook-stalk years later while clutching a glass of pinot grigio, looking at photos of him and his wife and children in matching Christmas pajamas.

I didn't even have sex until I was twenty years old (I made myself do it before turning twenty-one because the idea of waiting until I was of legal drinking age to fuck was just too sad to think about). I slept with a Russian guy named Lenny from Bensonhurst, Brooklyn who didn't really care if I was dead or alive but he made me laugh and we both liked the band Tool and we had a weird pseudo-flirtatious friendship so he seemed like a good candidate.

I lost my virginity on his bedroom floor while listening to Nine Inch Nails and it was about as terrible as it sounds.

By the time I was twenty-one, I guess the universe decided I was ready for an *actual* boyfriend when I met Harry* (we're going to use fake names throughout this book to protect the privacy of the guys I'm talking about, even though some of them truly deserve a Samantha Jones flyer moment—IYKYK). I dated Harry for seven long, tumultuous years. We fought like cats and dogs the majority of it. The relationship crashed and burned after a failed Paris proposal, intercepted by my extremely concerned family.

Then, on a bitter cold December night in 2009, I met my ex-husband, Julian*. We matched on a dating website (yes, website—this was when online dating was a *desktop experience*). When we "logged on" and emailed each other thoughtful messages on an actual computer, rather than lazily double-tapping an iPhone.

I was twenty-nine. I had just started my blog, *The Champagne Diet*, and was working my way up the corporate ladder at MTV. I can't tell you that I had any real goals in signing up for a dating site. I wasn't looking for a husband. I wasn't even looking for a serious relationship.

I remember telling a friend: *I just want to get dressed up and go on a date with a stranger.*

Julian and I shared our first kiss at midnight on New Year's Eve at a dive bar, just days after our first date. After that, we were inseparable. Within two months, he moved in.

We quickly settled into a life together. Weekends were cozy nights at home with red wine, Chinese food delivery, and movies. We talked about marriage early on and in an almost childlike way. *Marry me!* he'd say while we cuddled on the couch watching TV. I don't think either of us had any idea what the weight of being married held, but we were so obsessed with each other that we wanted to be as official as official gets.

One day at work, I was mindlessly scrolling TheKnot.com, as most girls in relationships do in their twenties. Between articles about engagement rings and "perfect" proposals, an ad caught my eye: *Win an Empire State Building Wedding With a View!*

I opened up a Word document and began casually writing an essay from my cubicle. *Our love is as timeless and iconic as that New York landmark*, I wrote while crushing a six-inch veggie sub and Diet Coke. I submitted the piece on a whim without telling anyone—not even Julian.

Three days later, I got a phone call from a publicist at The Knot. Out of tens of thousands of entries, fourteen couples had been selected to be married at the top of the Empire State Building on Valentine's Day 2011, and we were one of them.

I ran back to my desk and called Julian at work. "I have something to tell you," I giggled into the phone. "I entered a contest to win a Valentine's Day wedding at the Empire State Building, and we won…"

"No shit! That's awesome!" he replied.

"Wait, you think we should do it?" I asked.

"Hell yeah! This is amazing!" he said.

And just like that, I was engaged.

A little over three months later, we were married eighty-six stories above New York City in a beautiful ceremony at the top of the Empire State Building at sunset on February 14th, 2011. After a brutal winter, we got a surprise gorgeous sixty-degree day. Our wedding was featured in *The New York Daily News* complete with a full-page spread dedicated just for us. Everything about that time felt magical.

My first few years of marriage were pretty great. We did all the things new couples do: changed our Facebook status to *married*, spent quality time binge-watching reality TV together, and went on weekend getaways to the Hamptons. I added his last name to mine. We bought furniture from IKEA and drank cheap champagne while we assembled it. Ordered omelets on Sundays from the diner. Took a million selfies together.

Along with my new title of *wife*, I also took on the titles of *author* and *entrepreneur*. My blog was taking off, and I had started writing my first book—a lifelong dream. I was voraciously consuming personal development books, but I noticed a massive gap in the market. Everything felt out of touch, too buttoned-up, and definitely *not* for girls like me—women in their late twenties and early thirties who wore pink, drank white wine, and recognized Carrie Bradshaw as our patron saint. I had figured out how to live better, and I wanted to talk about the glittering power of mindset and manifestation with people who spoke the same language.

So, I enrolled in a life coaching program to help women beyond the blog and book. Once I was certified, I started taking on clients in the evenings and on weekends, juggling my full-time job at MTV with my coaching practice and book writing. *I loved to work.*

Julian supported my new business from the start. He spent long hours helping me build my website, self-publish my books, and navigate all the details I hadn't yet figured out. He was proud of me, as enthusiastic about my passions as I was. Whether it was carrying boxes of books to a signing, designing covers, or taking photos at my events, he wasn't just my husband—he was my biggest supporter.

But as the years passed and my career took off, we started drifting apart. I don't blame my business for it, but it was clear we were evolving in different directions. I was spending more time in the public eye—traveling for television appearances, book signings, speaking engagements—while he was happiest in the background. Julian had been a professional athlete in his twenties, and he had no desire for a life in the spotlight anymore. He preferred stability, routine, and quiet nights in. I thrived on movement, social energy, and saying yes to last-minute plans.

Slowly, we started living two separate lives.

Our dynamic was strange to most people, but I always defended it. And I always defended *him*. *He's just exhausted from work,* I'd tell friends who asked why he never came to parties. *The dog isn't feeling well, so he stayed back to keep an eye on him,* I'd explain to family members wondering why he wasn't at Thanksgiving dinner.

But if I was being honest, our dynamic was strange to *me* too. I just did what I always did—stuffed those feelings down and tried to ignore them. Julian was a *good* man, after all. But even though I was independent, even though I had gotten used to our way of doing things, I missed my husband. I wanted *more* time with him. I wanted him to come out with me. I wanted him to take me out. I wanted him to *want* me to stay home. I wanted a real marriage.

Our intimacy took a back seat during this time as well. I'd often ask him if we could plan a romantic night. He'd agree, but it never happened. Weeks without sex turned into months. Eventually, I stopped asking.

I oscillated between two feelings at all times: *this marriage isn't enough* and *I should be grateful for what I have.* I grew up believing that asking for too much was greedy, that wanting more meant being ungrateful. And wasn't that the truth about relationships? No one gets *everything.* Maybe I was just being unrealistic. Maybe I was expecting too much.

But there was another voice—a quieter one at first, but one that eventually refused to shut the fuck up—that told me the truth. *Neither of us were living authentically inside this marriage.*

I finally realized I wasn't asking for too much. I was just asking someone who could no longer give it to me.

I asked my husband for a divorce on January 1, 2020. And that, at least, he could give me.

After over ten years together—and just weeks before the world flipped on its head, throwing us into a global pandemic that would change everything—I became a divorcee. Of course, I didn't know what was coming. None of us did. But I knew one thing: I was turning forty, and I couldn't step into the next decade of my life trapped in a marriage that had run its course.

I wanted a chance to find a love that reflected who

I was—passionate, authentic, electric. I wanted to write a new chapter. I wanted to reinvent myself. *And maybe, finally, get laid again.*

So that winter, my husband and I split up. It was amicable, even peaceful. He moved out, and I stayed in our East Village apartment. I switched all the light bulbs to pink, reclaimed my closet space, and re-entered the dating world as a newly single, forty-year-old woman.

And what a world it was.

I quickly learned about things like *ghosting* and *situationships*—and I was truly horrified. I couldn't comprehend how someone could build a connection with you and then... *poof*—never speak to you again. Surely there had to be a logical explanation (like his untimely death?) preventing him from texting me back. But no, this motherfucker was out there, alive and well, with the absolute audacity to simply stop talking to me. *Mind! Blown!*

You mean to tell me I could go on one, two, even three dates with a man and he might still be seeing other women? I'm sorry, I don't really *grasp* the concept of a man *not* being instantly obsessed with me. And what the FUCK is a *roster*? The idea that a man could have sex with me and then send a text saying he didn't feel a "romantic vibe" makes me want to throw myself off a building—or worse—the idea that he could just... *evaporate* from my world, continue breathing air, and *not* want to marry me is disgusting.

Having only had two real relationships my entire adult life, you can see just how naive your girl was.

The past five years have been some of the most challenging of my life. Not just because of boy drama. But because relationships, if you let them, will teach you everything you never wanted to know about yourself. They illuminate your shadows, put your insecurities under a microscope, and hold up a mirror so unforgiving you have no choice but to look. And I had never looked at myself this much before.

I knew I had to document the massive shifts happening inside me. Even though I swore I'd never write about love, I couldn't stop the words from pouring out. I wasn't always getting it right. I picked the wrong guys more than once. I stayed too long most of the time. But through all of it, I was evolving. I was healing. I was learning. And even though it was nothing short of a complete and total shit show—every messy, beautiful second of it was mine.

What you're about to read in this book are some of the most real and raw words I've ever written. You're going to read about unrequited love, romantic delusions, divorce, cringe-worthy first dates, situationships, soul-shattering heartbreaks, hilarious WTF moments, and everything in between. You're getting the good, the bad, and the ugly. And man, there's a lot of ugly.

But there is also so much beauty. So much good. This path has forced me to unlock a completely different version of myself. And no, she isn't the same person she was. She's not supposed to be. She's better—so much better.

This book has been the hardest project of my life—both living it and writing it. But it has been totally worth it. Whether you're single, dating, trolling the apps, in a situationship, happily married, unhappily married, have a friend with benefits, keep going back to your ex, still missing your ex, in a happy relationship with someone fabulous, in a happy relationship with yourself, or some combination of any of those, my hope is that you'll see yourself in some of these stories. My hope is that you'll laugh at some of this. My hope is that you'll take some hope away from this.

My hope is that no matter what or *who* happens to you, you will never stop living with your heart cracked wide open.

CHAPTER ONE

MIAMI HEAT

When you're newly single and life has been a shit show, there's only one cure—Miami. Fortunately, one of my besties lives there, so I have a permanent invitation to soak up the sunshine and palm trees anytime I need an escape. So, I packed up my brightest dresses, got a spray tan, and headed south.

I should note, this much-needed trip came after nearly two years of pandemic living. I really don't want to spend too much energy writing about COVID, because I don't think any of us want to rehash that time, but I can't completely ignore it. We were all forced into quarantine just weeks after my divorce. Suddenly, I was living alone for the first time in a decade—which felt more like solitary confinement—processing the end of my marriage and the beginning of lockdown. I couldn't drown myself in dirty martinis or wear sparkly tops all around Manhattan. I couldn't go on flirty first dates in beautiful restaurants or dance till dawn with my girlfriends in sweaty clubs. Instead, I had to confront all my feelings head-on, locked inside an 11th-floor apartment in New York City that, although I was grateful for, started to feel like a bit of an insane asylum after a while.

Throw in the death of my estranged father—delivered via handwritten letter, no less—and, well, life was pretty fucking bleak. And oh yeah—I was about to turn forty! On April 23, 2020, my fortieth birthday, 2.7 million people in New York state were infected with COVID-19. 15,500 people had already died from the virus. So, 2020 wasn't really *my* year for more than a few reasons.

But back to a better topic—back to Miami.

My plane touched down in Magic City on a brisk March mid-week evening. I pulled up to the Ritz Carlton in Bal Harbour just in time to meet Kay, my friend and the business partner of my bestie, Tiffany, who *lives* in the hotel (yes, you read that correctly), for dinner. I decided to treat myself to the nicest hotel I could afford since I had been saving so much money over the past two years of doing absolutely nothing. So, The Ritz it was.

I checked in, left my luggage with the front desk, and slung my black leather motorcycle jacket over my shoulders to go meet Kay at the restaurant outside for a salmon Caesar salad and a nine-ounce pour of chardonnay (*never* get the six-ounce— just don't). The air was cool and energizing, a far cry from the frigid weather I had left behind in New York. I caught Kay up to speed on everything that had gone on in my life over the past two years while we chomped away at our salads.

Miami was interesting because it was almost like COVID never happened there. Between the laid-back laws and all the outdoor living, life looked and felt so different than it had in New York. I relished in the freedom and fresh air, and for the first time in a long time, I felt ready to let everything go and enjoy a long-overdue girls' weekend.

After our meal, I decided to head to my room and get some rest. I went to the front desk to grab my key card.

"Ms. Alwill, we have great news! We've decided to upgrade you to the Presidential Ocean View suite," the receptionist told me.

Holy shit.

"Wonderful," I said calmly, wondering how the hell my luck had shifted so quickly.

"Your bags are already upstairs. Juan will take you to your room."

Juan, who looked more like an extra in *Magic Mike XXL* than a bellboy, led me to the elevators and then up to my room on the top floor of the Ritz. He was muscular and bronzed, with a shiny shaved head and sparkling green eyes. He waved the key card in front of the door, and as soon as I heard the soft click of the lock, I took a deep breath.

The heavy wooden double doors opened, and an ice-cold

blast of air hit me as I walked into the largest, most gorgeous suite I'd ever seen in my life. I felt like *Little Orphan Annie* as Juan began the tour, leading me from room to room. My eyes widened as I took in the entryway, which was the size of a Manhattan studio apartment. He showed me the half bathroom, then we made our way to the living room area, which was filled with white and purple orchids and had more furniture than *all* my apartments I'd ever lived in combined. Sprawling couches, velvet chaises, and beautifully upholstered armchairs filled the space. To the right, a dining room with seating for six.

We made our way into the full open kitchen, decked out in white marble countertops and complete with top-of-the-line appliances—a dishwasher, stove, fridge, dinnerware, glassware—the works. *I mean, are you fucking kidding me?* Juan opened the giant sliding door, which took up the entire length of the living room, to reveal a breathtaking ocean view. I was in heaven.

Finally, he showed me the bedroom, which had its own private balcony, a spa bathroom, and walk-in closets. I thanked Juan, slapped a $20 in his palm, and walked him out. Then, I immediately ran to my luggage, pulled out my silky leopard pajama pants and a white tank top, and changed into my loungewear. I opened up my laptop, put on my Miami-themed Spotify playlist, and twirled across my suite into the kitchen. I found a split of champagne in the mini fridge, popped it open, poured a glass, and *took everything in.*

If the horror movie I had lived over the past few months was leading me to this moment, then I was okay with it.

The next day, Tiffany and I solidified our plans over the phone while I ate my room service egg-white omelet on my balcony in a hot pink kimono. Tiffany is the ultimate Miami ambassador. She's also a badass publicist who, along with whipping me up a last-minute press release whenever I need one, always gets us into the hottest spots, so I knew I was in good hands.

We met up at a Latin-Chinese fusion restaurant in Brickell with a few other girlfriends.

"We're gonna get Cara some D this weekend!" Tiffany shouted across the table as we all raised our cocktails in the air and toasted to her declaration. The neon fuchsia and purple strobe lights bounced off the walls as Doja Cat pumped through the restaurant.

After dinner, we went downtown to a bar that played old-school '90s and early '00s hip-hop—a crowd favorite of our crew. Get a bunch of girls together in their early forties, throw on some Lil' Kim, and suddenly, we're forgetting that we'll all need routine colonoscopies in a few years and instead reciting every line to *Crush On You* like it's 1996 and we're rocking our Knicks starter jackets to a house party in Brooklyn.

We walked in and found a high-top table to post up at. We ordered our drinks as "Juicy" by Biggie blared in the background. Tiffany shot me her famous wink and smirk.

"Having fun, boo?" she asked me, bumping her hip against mine.

"The best time. I needed this," I told her, tilting my head back and emptying a golden glass of champagne down my throat.

"Look at that hottie over there." Tiffany pointed to a tall, olive-skinned, bearded guy in the corner wearing a Yankees hat. "He keeps staring at you!" she said, pawing my arm.

"Oh my GOD," I whispered. He was *gorgeous.* I blushed and looked away when we caught eyes.

"Go talk to him!" Tiffany urged.

"No way. The man has to chase the woman," I explained. I had been reading all the classic dating manuals for the first time ever, and according to my new bible, *Why Men Love Bitches*, "Anything a person chases in life runs away." I recited this to our table like it was scripture.

I remained perched at my spot like a Good Bitch, sipping my bubbly, watching group after group of women approach this beautiful mystery man. Every time new girls left his table after unsuccessfully hooking him, he'd look over to check on me. It was clear *these bitches* hadn't read the book.

Our eye contact grew more and more intense. Soon, he smiled at me.

"Girl! Go get your man!" shouted Tiffany as she returned to our table with tequila shots. "He's *so* into you!"

"Tiffany, I am *not* approaching him," I explained. "It's

Attraction Principle #16. He has to come to *me*." Tiffany rolled her eyes and took a sip of her drink.

Within minutes, Yankee Hat and his wingman got up and moved to our table. "Hey you," he said as he pulled up a bar stool and sat close to me. "I'm Jacob." He stretched his arm out to shake my hand.

"I'm Cara," I said, raising my glass to his. "Nice to meet you!"

We started chatting and he told me he was from New York and had been living in Miami most of his life. Miami is *filled* with New York transplants, and can you blame them? Trading rat-filled sidewalks for sun-soaked sand didn't seem like such a bad idea, especially at this moment. I didn't quite understand what he did for a living, but that's typical Miami. Something about traveling the world, managing rich people's money— I didn't know and I didn't care. This man was hot as hell and I was just happy to bask in the attention.

We talked for a few more minutes and then I suddenly felt a jolt of electricity zap through my whole body as he placed his hand on mine. He then gently grabbed the side of my jaw with his other hand and pulled me in for a kiss. Within seconds we were in a full-fledged make-out session; our faces buried in each other, both of his hands now in my hair. I could taste the tequila on his tongue as he gently bit my bottom lip.

"You are *so* gorgeous," he growled.

Tiffany signaled to me that she was leaving and gave me

a thumbs up and raised her eyebrows, the kind of check-in someone makes when they know they need to leave you alone, but want to make sure you're okay. I gave her a thumbs up behind Jacob's head as he ran his hands all over my thighs, creeping up my caramel-colored silk slip dress.

"Should we get out of here?" he whispered into my ear.

This is the point I need to admit to you, dear reader, that I had never, in the entirety of my life, taken a stranger home with me. I had never had a one-night stand.

"I'm staying at the Ritz. Come back with me," I whispered back as I kissed his neck. Blame it on the champagne or the universe pushing me to finally let go, but that night, I was a woman possessed. Hot, in control, and reckless in the best way. And I *liked* it.

"I'll get us an Uber," he said. "Let me go pay the bill."

I slung my metallic gold Chanel purse across my shoulder, stood up, and straightened out my dress. My mind was spinning. *Was I actually about to do this? How does it all work? Would he have condoms? Did I remember to shave?* I ran my hand down the side of my calf to make sure my legs were smooth. He grabbed my hand and led me out the door. A black Chevy Suburban pulled up and he opened the door for me as I climbed inside.

We made out for the whole thirty-minute Uber ride back to my hotel. The champagne and tequila blurred my memory somewhat, but I can tell you that we certainly had sex and

I certainly made him leave afterward so I could have my pristine, California King bed all to myself. I'm not sure where I had cultivated my newfound audacity, but I loved it.

I woke up in the morning in nothing but my black lace thong. I surveyed the room and found all sorts of clothes strewn around the bathroom floor. My pajamas, a bathrobe, my bra, the dress I had on the night before. A full, untouched glass of champagne was on my nightstand.

I felt like a fucking goddess.

A reminder from my Delta app flashed across my phone. *Flight DL423 to New York is on time.* Shit. I had two hours to pack and get to the airport. I quickly picked everything off the floor and shoved all my wrinkled clothes into my pink Away suitcase. I took a fast shower, slapped on some tinted moisturizer and concealer, and hastily sprayed my Tom Ford Black Orchid perfume in the hopes of masking the smell of alcohol seeping out of my pores. I headed downstairs to soak up a few final moments of sunshine before leaving to catch my flight.

As I tried my best to choke down a cup of coffee and fight off my raging hangover under the swaying palms, Yankee Hat sent a text: *I had a great time with you. Have a safe flight! Next time let's do this the right way. Dinner when you're back?*

Definitely. I replied.

The truth was, I didn't care whether I saw him again or not. I didn't need to have dinner with him. Or jump into a long-distance love affair. Yankee Hat had given me a gift that night. He reminded me that I was sexy. He reminded me that I was desirable. He awoke something inside of me that had been dormant for far too long.

And on that steamy Miami morning, that was more than enough. And for the first time in a long time, so was I.

CHAPTER TWO

YOU'VE GOT MALE

My life changed forever in 1996 when AOL introduced a monthly flat fee of $19.95 for unlimited internet access. Suddenly my time online was no longer being micromanaged by my single mom who constantly balanced letting my brother and I explore the world wide web at an exorbitant hourly rate with us not getting evicted. Expensive internet access for two curious, horny teenagers was a recipe for bankruptcy. The biggest perk of unlimited access for me: I could hang out in chat rooms for as long as I wanted.

Chat rooms were heaven for me. Around 10 p.m. each night, I'd turn off all the lights in our living room once my mom and brother went to sleep and pop into rooms with names like "Brooklyn Skateboarders M4F" or "Punk Rock and Tattoo Talk." With nothing but the glow of our Gateway computer monitor illuminating my cherubic teenaged face, I'd immediately scroll the list of screen names looking for anyone that seemed like they could be a boy.

"A/S/L?" I'd type to anyone with a name that included words like "punk" or "skater" in them. It was so freeing to chat with guys online. Suddenly all of my insecurities were gone. I could rely strictly on my quick wit and musical knowledge and not worry about whether or not the boys I was talking to would think I was fat or realize that I was sitting there in an oversized Smashing Pumpkins *Melancholy and The Infinite Sadness* t-shirt with marinara sauce stains on it. Fantasy reigned supreme online and I was there for it.

I had one type and one type only—a guy who loved the same bands as me. Bonus points if he rode a skateboard. Double bonus points if he had tattoos.

I met Ray inside of a "New York City Tattoo" chat room two years later in 1998. I asked the room if anyone had advice for someone getting their first tattoo, which was at the very top of my goal list for that year now that I was finally eighteen. Ray IM'd me outside of the chat so we could talk privately and I learned that he was from The Bronx, he was the lead singer in a ska band, and he had tattoos—lots of them. We exchanged photos and once we established we were both attracted to each other enough through our grainy, scanned 4x6 digital prints, our IMs turned into phone calls.

I talked to Ray for weeks on my see-through clear plastic phone on my private landline in my bedroom. With every conversation, the anticipation built and I started liking him more and more. Our relationship was entirely phone-based and

I started to wonder if we'd ever meet up in real life, until one day he invited me on a double date with his best friend Sam. Sam was the drummer in Ray's band, and the plan was for me to bring a friend for him and we'd all go to the movies and have dinner together afterward at Applebee's. This was the moment of truth. The first blind meeting; the moment I'd know if my AOL boyfriend and I would translate IRL.

Ray pulled up to my apartment building on a Saturday afternoon in his teal Nissan Sentra. Sam was in the front seat. My friend and I hid out in anticipation behind the frosted glass doors of my lobby as they parked in the bus stop. Ray looked different in person; paler, pudgier, and balder. I was immediately sad. We gave each other a friendly hug, carried on with our double date, and never hung out again.

I bounced back quickly, and for a few more years, I racked up a roster of chat room boyfriends—most of whom I never met in real life. But none of that mattered. Chat room boyfriends were pure fantasy for me, and back then, that was all I really needed.

I know without a doubt that chat rooms were my gateway drug to dating apps years later. Now older, I was ready for the real deal. The idea that my computer—and now my phone—held a world of men inside it, each one with the potential to be *The One*, was thrilling. I wouldn't be single for long after my divorce. All I had to do was download Hinge, the dating app 'designed to be deleted,' and my next romance would be waiting for me at the click of a button.

I quickly realized I had made one fatal error when creating my first Hinge profile—I told the truth.

I remember proudly uploading my photos, similar to the ones I shared on Instagram, highlighting not just myself but my biggest milestones, especially in my work. One of the photos I was most excited to include was a shot of me standing in the middle of Times Square, in front of a billboard with my face on it. An ad I had taken out to promote my podcast, *Style Your Mind*, which had just surpassed ten million downloads. I uploaded the photo and paired it with the pre-written caption: *As seen on my mom's fridge.*

I answered the prompts with honesty and confidence. Under *My Proudest Accomplishment*, I wrote: *Getting to wake up every day without an alarm clock and do what I love.* I shared that I was an author and an entrepreneur, and that I had quit my full-time job years ago to pursue my business. I finished filling out the rest of my profile, hit publish, and then—crickets.

A few guys liked me that week, but not one of them was remotely my type or seemed to have anything in common with me. I couldn't understand what was going on. I felt like a catch! My photos were cute and clear, and I had thoughtfully written about myself and what I was looking for—either a long-term or short-term relationship (I knew enough to stay far away from the term *life partner*).

It was time to take matters into my own hands. I ditched the *Why Men Love Bitches* mentality, poured myself a glass of wine, and became the hunter. I'm a boss bitch, after all. I don't sit around waiting for things to happen in my business, so why would I wait around for a man to find me on the internet? If I want to accomplish something, I work my ass off until it happens. Dating would be no different.

At first, I was picky, only liking guys who seemed like someone I could really see myself with. But an hour and two glasses of red wine later, my standards became a bit less rigid. *I guess I could have a drink with him*, I rationalized, staring at a photo of a cop from Queens who may or may not have had a broken tooth.

Bloop! My phone sounded. A match—and a message—from a cute, tattooed journalist named Matthew who lived in Brooklyn. I squealed and immediately opened the app.

○ **Matthew:** Hey Cara

○ **Me:** Hey Matthew! I see you live in Brooklyn. I grew up there :)

○ **Matthew:** Oh cool! I grew up in Boston.

○ **Me:** Nice.

○ **Matthew:** Tell me about what you do?

○ **Me:** I'm an author and a coach for women entrepreneurs. I also have a podcast. I own a global female empowerment brand. Tell me about your journalism world!

Matthew never replied.

This type of experience was typical on the apps. It seemed like any time I mentioned what I did for a living, my electronic future boyfriend either turned into a ghost or worse, made a weird comment like, *Oh wow. You're way cooler than me.* Then I'd spend the next few minutes downplaying my accomplishments and building up his ego.

The only men who seemed confident were the ones who had nothing to lose and just wanted to get laid. I thought I was making headway with an artist named Doug—until the day of our date arrived and he told me his dog was sick, asking if we could just have drinks at his place.

I don't really feel comfortable going to your place on a first date, I explained.

He waited three hours to respond before finally saying, *I'm sorry. I can't make it tonight. I think we're looking for different things.*

Things felt bleak. I missed my AOL chat room days—where, somehow, I'd had more luck as an eighteen-year-old college student than I did as a highly accomplished woman in her early forties. And I wasn't alone. I'd had countless conversations with girlfriends who were experiencing the exact same thing.

I was so curious that I started doing research. *Are men freaked out by successful women?* I typed into Google.

That's when I came across a book called *The Love Gap* by Jenna Birch, which asked that exact question. From the book's Amazon description:

Modern men claim to want smarts, success, and independence in romantic partners. Or so says the data collected by scientists and dating websites. If that's the case, why are so many independent, successful women winning in life, but losing in love? Journalist Jenna Birch has finally named the perplexing reason: "the love gap"—or that confusing rift between who men say they want to date and who they actually commit to. Backed by extensive data, research, in-depth interviews with experts and real-life relationship stories, The Love Gap is the first book to explore the most talked-about dating trend today.

I downloaded the book to my Kindle app and began devouring it. Sadly, all that data, research, and in-depth interviews confirmed what I had feared—men loved the *idea* of a smart woman, but when it came down to it, most of them didn't actually want to be with one.

One night, while enjoying my usual dinner of chardonnay and Skinny Pop popcorn (*white cheddar flavor, always*), I remembered the *Sex and the City* episode where Miranda goes speed dating. The moment she shared that she was an attorney, her dates lost interest. So she tried an experiment—rather than saying she was a lawyer, she told them she was a flight attendant. Suddenly, men were falling all over her, begging to take her out.

I cued up the episode and watched it again for inspiration. Brilliant.

Immediately, I opened my Hinge profile and, in my Kendall Jackson Chardonnay haze, changed *everything*. I deleted any mention of what I did for a living. Kept my prompt responses short and bubbly. Softened my sentences with smiley faces. Swapped my photos for sexier ones—me looking playful at parties, me in a tight, body-hugging dress.

I had, essentially, rebranded myself into a dumb blonde. Just to see what would happen.

And the next morning? I woke up to nearly 150 likes.

I wound up securing a handful of dates with guys I was actually excited about. I wasn't lying about who I was—I figured I'd just share more details about myself once we were in person. Lure them in with my boobs and charm, then drop the bomb that I wasn't exactly planning to be barefoot and pregnant.

Eliminating the opportunity for them to have any preconceived notions about me felt like a genius move.

And then, I met them.

There was Kyle, the kindergarten teacher who tried to bang me in the bathroom of a karaoke bar. Dustin, the recovering alcoholic who I'm certain showed up drunk to our date (*that, or he was just truly out of his mind*). Jim, the failing comedian who carried a mini bottle of rum in his pocket and asked me to split the $17 bill for the food truck tacos we shared.

The matches I made while *hiding myself* were exhausting. I knew that by omitting the things that made me *me*, I was blocking myself from meeting the kind of man who could— and *wanted*—to handle me.

All of me.

A few weeks later, I deleted Hinge.

It turns out, being a dumb blonde was just too much work.

MY BUMBLE PROFILE

PERFECT FIRST DATE

The one where I don't know that you texted your ex-girlfriend three days ago because you're still in love with her. The one where you don't know that I act like a psychotic bitch the week before my period and will pick fights with you out of thin air just to make sure you still love me. The one where I don't know how many random women in bikinis you follow on Instagram. The one where you haven't seen me drunk-eat Cheetos and wipe the orange dust on my pajama bottoms. The one where I don't know that it's nearly impossible for you to get hard without Viagra because of your crippling anxiety. The one where you don't know that I have severe abandonment issues and will assume you hate me if you take more than thirty minutes to reply to my text.

The one where we're both still pretending.

I GET WAY TOO EXCITED ABOUT

That moment when I come home from a *grueling* day of walking three blocks to Whole Foods for my overpriced, organic 365-brand pre-cut vegetables, only to immediately rip my bra off before I even make it to my bedroom. The feeling of letting my big titties breathe is indescribable. Why do I even need to wear a bra in the first place? Isn't it annoying that flat-chested women can go braless without controversy, but when I do it, it's considered offensive? This is the same reason I could never get away with a "cheeky bottom" bathing suit. My ass is fat. And while big asses are trendy these days, I can't just *swing it around* on the beach without getting looks.

So yeah, I get excited about letting all my shit loose in the privacy of my own home.

A PRO AND CON OF DATING ME

Pro: I make a mean lasagna.

Con: I will torture you over the fact that you have loved and had sex with other women before me.

AFTER WORK, YOU CAN FIND ME

Slowly draining a bottle of red wine alone on my couch, in the same sweatpants I've been wearing for five days, listening to music exclusively made before 2001.

I'M A GREAT PLUS ONE BECAUSE

I will spend hundreds of dollars to look absolutely stunning, never give you shit for introducing me to everyone as *your friend*, and then still have sex with you afterward.

IF I COULD EAT ONE MEAL FOR THE REST OF MY LIFE, IT WOULD BE

A 1:45 a.m. delivery of emotional support mozzarella sticks, grilled cheese, and cheese fries from Remedy Diner. Paired with *yet another* glass of pinot noir that I absolutely do *not* need after drinking my way through the East Village for the past six hours. But I'll pour it anyway.

I will take exactly two sips before eating the entire grilled cheese, two and a half mozzarella sticks, and zero fries.

The next morning, I'll wake up to a Spotify playlist blasting, Bravo muted on the TV, and the remnants of my meal on the kitchen counter. There will be clues before I even get out of bed—ketchup on my t-shirt, a rogue, stale french fry in my sheets.

I will absolutely eat the french fry.

I will check my phone to make sure I didn't send any inappropriate drunk texts to a man who does not want me. Then I will walk into the kitchen and battle the overwhelming wave of shame by replacing it with grace, *just as my Zoom therapist taught me.* I will swear that I'm going on a diet and *not eating for the rest of the day.*

I will crack by 11 a.m. and rationalize that I *need* a turkey bacon, egg, and cheese on a toasted everything bagel (*scooped out, of course*) to cure my hangover. I will drink too much coffee and soothe my raging hangxiety with a glass of champagne by 1 p.m.

I will have three glasses.

And I will do this all over again next weekend.

CHAPTER THREE

THE JUKEBOX IS BROKEN

Rick and I matched on Hinge on Valentine's Day. Absolute cringe, I know. A few days later, on an icy February evening, I found myself power-walking down Avenue A in a leopard-print faux fur coat, my frozen hands clutching it closed, on my way to our first date at an East Village dive bar.

You didn't think I could really stay off those apps, did you?

Rick had told me to pick the place. I chose this one because, first of all—I love a dive bar. The lighting was moody and candlelit. They served decent wine. And it had a jukebox, which I had mentioned was one of my favorite things in my newly revamped dating profile.

While en route, I got a text from Rick: *The jukebox is broken.*

I walked in and spotted him hovering near a high-top table in the back. He was tall and broad, with a thick black beard. Hotter in real life than he was in his photos. A phenomenon that has happened in the history of *never* when it comes to online dating. He wore black work boots and a hoodie with a blazer over it.

We hugged tightly, his smile genuine, relieved—like, *thank God you're not a monster.* I felt the same.

The date lasted five hours. We never ran out of things to say. We made each other laugh. We even flirted a bit. He told me about the audition he had gone on that morning (he was an actor, or at least trying to become one), and I told him about my writing career.

The next morning, he texted me to say he had a great time. So, naturally, I assumed—as most red-blooded American women do—that he was in love with me.

Then, radio silence. Days passed with no word from Rick. *Could he be dead?* I genuinely wondered.

Finally, a full week later, his name popped up on my phone at 6:45 p.m. on a Friday.

💬 **Rick:** Hey, what are you up to tonight?

I told him I was free (rookie mistake—apparently, being available at all hours is not sexy or mysterious?). I also assumed he'd ask to hang out. But no. Rick never asked me out. Instead, he just started narrating his night in excruciating detail and told me he was perusing Seamless because he wanted to order a milkshake and drink it in bed.

A milkshake.

I asked if he wanted to grab a drink.

○ **Rick:** It's too cold to go out.

At this point, most women would have emotionally checked out. Maybe even blocked him. But not me! No, no. This was the precise moment I morphed from a beautiful, smart woman into a dog with a bone. Rick was now a challenge. And I was going to make him want me more than he wanted that damn milkshake.

Rick resurfaced via text the following week—this time, *actually* asking me out. He invited me to get breakfast and walk around the city that weekend.

I love a day date. It's a great way to confirm two things: 1) That they are still attractive in the daylight and 2) That they are not a raging alcoholic.

A lot of men are raging alcoholics. Especially in New York City.

Plus, I have this theory that almost anyone can fall in love at night after a few drinks in a dimly lit bar, so I was thrilled that Rick and I still hit it off over coffee and bagels on a bench in Washington Square Park. We kissed at the end of the date and the chemistry was there. It was official: I had a crush.

Then came another Friday night text that led nowhere.

For two painful hours, we exchanged the most mind-numbing small talk while I sat on my couch in pajamas, slurping down red wine and listening to The Smiths (*can you imagine a more depressing scene?*). Somewhere around glass number three, I got bold.

○ **Me:** So are you coming over or what?

○ **Rick:** Give me an hour.

And that, my friends, was the beginning of what I call my Soft Whore Era.

I was older, wiser, and hornier. Starving for sexual attention after my divorce (followed by a year of quarantine). If I wasn't finding my next boyfriend, I was at least going to get laid. But I couldn't fully commit to being a true whore. So this was my *Soft Whore Era*—a baby step into the world of casual sex.

Rick showed up exactly one hour later at 10 p.m. on the dot. I was in leggings and a cropped Blondie sweatshirt, another glass of wine deep. I asked if he wanted anything to drink.

Rick: Do you have a soda?

Because I am a single New York City woman, the only liquids in my home were water, wine, and coffee. I dug a months-old White Claw out of the back of my fridge.

Me: This work?

Rick shrugged and took it.

We moved to the couch. I handed him the remote because he was tall and manly, and that just felt like the right thing to do. He put on a stand-up comedy special and we started making out.

Between kisses, we cuddled but barely spoke. Rick was glued to the TV. I was glued to the bulge in his crotch. Things got intense, but he never pushed for more. I wasn't about to initiate, because in my mind, I am still an awkward teenager terrified of rejection.

He left at 4 a.m. I was *convinced* he was in love with me.

The next morning, I recounted the entire night to my girl-friends via voice notes the length of a podcast. We all came to the same conclusion that Rick was really into me. Spoiler alert: he was not.

Rick continued texting me once a week with riveting messages like: "Hey kid" and "Sup?" and I waited for those texts. Obsessed over them. Promptly screenshotted them to every single girlfriend who was invested in my imaginationship.

By May, we had hung out one more time—another couch makeout session. We still hadn't had sex. I felt like a cat in heat.

Then, one Saturday morning, he texted first. This had never happened. So surely, this meant we were inching toward a relationship.

We started sexting. Well, he sexted. I mostly fumbled through it. I even Googled *hottest sext messages to send a guy* (pro tip: don't do that).

By dinnertime, I just thought, fuck it.

💬 **Me:** So who's getting in the Uber, me or you?

💬 **Rick:** You.

I took an Everything Shower (shaved, exfoliated, and lotioned), put on my best *sexy yet effortless* outfit, and called an Uber Black to Jersey City (yes, Jersey City honey). Thirty min-utes later, I was standing at his door.

I wish I could say I was channeling my most empowered Samantha Jones self as I pulled up in a Suburban to the house of a man who hadn't even asked me on a third date. But the truth is, I just wanted to be wanted.

Rick met me at the front door and led me upstairs to the top floor of his two-story rental. He gave me a grand tour, which began in the living room, where there was nothing but a recliner and a massive television set.

We moved to the bedroom, which was equally sparse. A full-sized bed, a TV, and a wooden dresser. That was it. He turned off the lights, put on a horror movie, and patted the bed for me to get in. *Not creepy at all.*

We laid down, spooning while I faced the TV. He started kissing the back of my neck, and within minutes, both of our clothes were off. That's when things got…weird.

The sex was silent. Like, disturbingly silent. No sounds. No words. Nothing.

At one point, while switching positions, he accidentally head-butted me. Normally, this would be the kind of thing that makes you both burst into laughter, but instead, he just kept going like it never happened.

The only thing more alarming than the complete lack of noise was the *sheer size* of his dick—which, in theory, sounds like a win.

It was not.

I tried to make some noise just to fill the void, but I felt like I was having sex in a library. I don't know if he was *concentrating* or *dissociating*, but the whole thing felt less like sex and more like a trip to the DMV.

When it was over, I got dressed immediately. We laid there for another hour in the dark, on opposite sides of the bed, watching more stand-up comedy in complete silence. Which, given what just happened, felt appropriate.

At 2 a.m., I ordered an Uber back to the city.

A week passed before I heard from him again.

○ **Rick:** Sorry, I'm not ignoring you. I lost my phone. And my bank card. And my job.

I'm pretty sure the dog ate his homework too.

I never saw Rick again.

CHAPTER FOUR

WHY ARE MY LIPS NUMB?

O nce upon a time, I developed a *Jordan Catalano-level* crush on a man named Matteo. He was painfully cool, self-absorbed beyond comprehension, and hot as hell—but not in a classic way. He reeked of patchouli and chaos and had the rare ability to make me feel like I was both the only woman on the planet and simultaneously nonexistent.

Matteo owned a bar in the East Village where I lived, and I'd see him around the neighborhood fairly often. We made heavy eye contact every time we crossed paths. Once, he almost crashed his skateboard into a parked car because he was too busy turning his head to check me out while I walked down Avenue B. We had this *thing* even though we had never formally met.

Then, one chilly October afternoon, I was home, nursing a cold, scrolling Hinge in my pajamas. Dating apps had become my go-to whenever I needed a hit, though the whole thing felt so counterintuitive because all I ever got was disappointment after disappointment. Were these apps designed to match you with the absolute worst people possible just to keep you coming back for more? At this point, I was beginning to think so. But then, something magical happened. Just when I was convinced Hinge was failing miserably at its one job, it matched me with Matteo.

I had liked him first, adding a cute comment about us living in the same neighborhood. He matched with me a few hours later, and we started chatting, both pretending we had no idea who the other was. After a few days of messaging back and forth, he finally wrote: *So what do you say we get a drink on Friday night, neighbor? ;)*

Two nights later, I was floating down Avenue B, on my way to my date with my longtime crush. I had curated the perfect first-date outfit: a black slip dress, a fitted motorcycle jacket with my crystal Chanel brooch attached, and white Converse. This would become my official F.D.O. (First Date Outfit). I walked into the bar and spotted Matteo perched on a stool, chatting up a stranger. Of course, he was talking to someone. He was so cool.

"Bella!" he said the moment he saw me, arms outstretched. He pulled me into a tight hug, and that—right then—was the precise moment I sold my soul to the devil. God, he smelled good. God, he *looked* good.

I hopped onto the barstool next to him and immediately began nervously rambling about my walk over and a series of other completely unimportant things: "A rat ran right past my feet on my way here! I'm still shaking! Isn't it beautiful out tonight? We got so lucky with this weather today! How was your day?" *My god, Cara. Shut the fuck up.*

He reached for my hands and squeezed them. A few seconds passed before I realized he wasn't letting go. My stomach fluttered. My face grew hot. I swear, I could have melted right into that barstool. Actually, *that* was the moment I sold my soul to the devil.

The conversation blurred. And then, he kissed me. This wasn't just any kiss. It was the kind of kiss where the world slows down, where you forget anyone else exists, where your mind floats up toward the ceiling like a balloon. Where was I? Who was I? Did it matter? Matteo and I were making out in a dark East Village bar, and nothing else mattered.

We stayed for an hour, kissing and talking, and then he suggested we grab another drink at his bar. That was all it took for me to begin immediately imagining our life together. The East Village's favorite power couple: the edgy bar owner and the cute writer chick. I imagined myself moving into his apartment—it only made sense, he lived right above the bar. I pictured myself coming downstairs every evening around happy hour with my laptop to sit at the bar and write while he poured drinks for the college kids who flooded in for cheap beer. He'd wink at me from across the bar while I worked on my next book. Locals would come in and greet both of us.

Girls would walk in and be jealous of me.

Matteo paid the bill as I reached for my purse. I pointed to his phone, reminding him he was about to forget it on the bar. He grabbed his phone in one hand, my hand in the other, and we walked out the door. We giggled and kissed the entire four-block walk to his bar.

"Head to the back and get whatever you want. Don't you dare pay for anything. Tell them you're with me. I'll be right back." And then, he vanished. For what felt like six hours. Okay, it was twenty minutes, but still.

I got antsy waiting and finally walked toward the entrance for fresh air. As I stepped outside, I heard a loud thud and turned to see him closing the door to his apartment building. "I'm back! I'm so sorry it took me so long!" he said.

He was in a completely different outfit. Now he was wearing distressed white jeans, a Hawaiian shirt, and a fedora. "Why did you change?" I asked, puzzled.

"You just looked so fancy! I felt underdressed."

I smiled. He pulled me in for another kiss. And that's when my lips went numb.

"Why are my lips numb!?" I asked, cackling, because after four glasses of wine, I found this hilarious.

"Oh, I did a bump, babe. Want some?"

"No thanks!" I said casually, as if he was offering me a sip of his seltzer and not cocaine.

He suggested we go back to my place to chill out and listen

to music, and that was music to my ears. We got to my apartment, I put on one of my favorite playlists—The Strokes, New Order, The Smiths—kicked off my Converse, and waltzed into the kitchen. I swung open the fridge, grabbed a bottle of Moët, and held up an empty wine glass.

"Some *champagne* with your *cocaine*?" I giggled.

I don't know why I found his coke habit funny, or why I was so unbothered by the fact that I'd just invited a man I barely knew to do drugs in my home like it was some kind of late '90s afterparty for two. That night, we made out some more. He told me he'd had a crush on me for years from seeing me around the neighborhood. Then he told me he loved me. Then he cried.

I knew it was bizarre to have a man profess his love to me on a first date. Was he love bombing me? Was he trying to get me to sleep with him? Was he insane? Or was this fate? Psychics would call it a past-life connection. Therapists would call it trauma bonding. Were we two fucked-up kids, desperate for connection? Were we soulmates, destined to reunite across timelines?

Or were we just... wasted?

Probably all of the above.

CHAPTER FIVE

SPELLBOUND

"**C**ara, it looks like you're holding a fucking vigil in here," my friend Jenn said as she walked into my apartment.

"These are the love candles I told you about!" I yelled from the kitchen while putting together a cheese plate for us.

Jenn stared at the four tall prayer candles burning in a row on my desk, glitter etched into their wax, glowing like the votive stand of St. Patrick's Cathedral. Except a little creepier.

One of them was red, with a black and purple spider web design. Another was white, with pink and blue hearts. The third was red with a glittery pentagram, and the fourth, pink, covered in even more hearts. Each candle had a name taped to the bottom, handwritten in cursive, marking its purpose. Today, I was working with *Spellbound: Come To Me*—the candle meant to attract your lover instantly.

"Remember I told you about High Priestess Selene, the Witch Queen of New York City?" I shouted.

"Um, no. I think I would have remembered that," Jenn called back.

"I was picking up a plant the other day at the flower shop and I saw her love candles and decided to grab one," I explained as I walked into the living room, carrying a tray of aged gouda and manchego on my You're a Mess ceramic platter—an impulse buy from a neighborhood gift shop.

"I'm telling you, I hadn't heard from Matteo in seven days. I lit this candle, Jenn, and he texted me within two hours," I said carefully, like I was presenting forensic evidence.

My preoccupation with Matteo was turning me into a complete psychopath. Our first date had ended with him telling me he was in love with me. Then he disappeared for a week. I was so sure he was dead that I actually walked by his bar in a giant faux fur coat and oversized Chloé sunglasses (clearly in disguise, but also, not at all because this is just how I actually dress). I stood behind a tree across the street and peered in. I didn't see him, but convinced myself he had to be alive because surely the bar would have been closed down for mourning if the owner had died, right?

Eventually, Matteo resurfaced. We hung out again. And then, like clockwork, he disappeared. For ten more days. It became a cycle. Rinse, repeat. Another emotionally unavailable man I had attached myself to, who clearly had no idea that his inconsistency and general disregard for my well-being had me performing full-fledged witchcraft rituals just to lure him into texting me.

Jenn picked up one of the candles and turned it upside down. "Lover Return to Me? Uncrossing? Love Healing? What the fuck is this?"

"I'm telling you. We were suddenly talking every day again, then the candle burned out and I didn't have a chance to pick up a new one and—poof!—he was gone. As soon as I bought another, he came back. It's magical," I said.

"No, it's dysfunctional," Jenn said. "But do I need one?"

My fascination with all things mystical goes back to childhood. I have always been obsessed with tarot readers, the occult, and the seduction of the spiritual world. In junior high, I became consumed by the Salem Witch Trials and read about them every chance I got. My best friend had an aunt who lived in her basement and was a Stevie Nicks doppelgänger. She had long, blonde hair, pointy red nails, and wore black velvet capes while burning incense. I was infatuated with her.

I loved watching infomercials for psychic hotlines, enamored by the readers who promised that if you just *CALLED NOW!* they could tell you everything you needed to know about the future. I became so captivated by the spiritual realm that when I was fourteen, I saw an infomercial claiming you could train to become a psychic—and immediately heeded the call. I dialed the 1-900 number on the screen and ordered the free manual that promised to help me build a fortune-telling business from home.

When the book arrived, my mother found it and quickly realized the training was dual-purpose. You could become a psychic, or a phone sex operator. *For maximum income.* She threw it in the trash and banned me from ever pulling a stunt like that again.

As I got older, I would seek out tarot readers and mediums both in person and online. If someone wanted to channel my spirit guides, I was game. Tell me *everything.* I loved daydreaming about the unknown. And I loved that the occult provided something that was often hard to find within ourselves—it provided *hope.*

Jenn and I cackled as I pulled two champagne coupes from my cupboard and poured us drinks.

"So, what's up with Matteo? Have you guys hung out recently?" she asked.

"No, I haven't seen him in a few weeks, but he's been really busy opening his new bar. He checks in with me. I also think maybe he's drinking. You know, all the stress. He's burned out. Poor guy has a lot going on," I told her.

I, like most women, possess the incredibly convenient gift of spinning a storyline about a man to fit whatever mood I'm in and whatever reality I want to experience. This week, Matteo was *The Good Guy.* Last week, he was a *raging cokehead in desperate need of inner-child healing.* My friends somehow knew how to keep up.

But Matteo just had that *thing* about him. He smelled

intoxicating, owned a bar, rode a skateboard. He was passionate, aloof, and sexy as hell. When I was with him, it felt like the world stopped. Sure, he had a small drug problem and was most likely an alcoholic, but I *wanted* him.

If I could bottle up the electricity between us and sell it to women everywhere, I'd be a *fucking gazillionaire*. There was something about him—or *us*—that was *charged*. I later learned from a therapist that those *sparks* are actually anxiety, that my body was *warning* me, that my nervous system was going haywire because it felt unsafe. But *damn*, I felt alive around this dude.

After Jenn left that weekend, I started thinking about my addiction to emotionally unavailable men. It had been this way since my first serious relationship in my early twenties. My first boyfriend, Harry, used to disappear constantly. I'd spend days waiting by the phone, willing him to call me back. And when he finally resurfaced, the *high* I felt was indescribable.

Looking back, it's clear that in nearly every relationship, I felt like I needed to work overtime to be noticed, acknowledged, and loved. This is usually the formula for a little girl whose dad left, ya know? Mine also happened to be on drugs. Something happens to you when the first man who is supposed to love you *takes off*. You're never the same.

I had perfected the art of attracting—and *entertaining*—the most difficult men on the planet. Addicts. Narcissists. Players. Users. But ultimately, the storyline was the same. A tale as old as time. A girl in love with being unloved.

Matteo and I continued to see each other for the next few months, and my obsession only grew stronger. I spent my days staring at my phone, waiting for that hit, defending him to all my girlfriends who hated his guts for treating me like an option. I didn't care. Even though I wanted all of him, a piece of him was better than nothing.

By Christmas, Matteo and I hadn't seen each other in a month. He sent me a text on Christmas Eve that simply said, *Merry Christmas, Cara!* which I read as wedding vows. That three-word text made me far happier than it should have, but by then, I had become so accustomed to his breadcrumbing that when he did reach out, my whole body reacted. It was that rush, that dopamine hit I *desperately* needed.

I was an addict, just like him.

When the new year rolled around, I decided I needed to make some big changes in my life. I hated how powerless I felt when it came to men. I had it all together—like I always did— when it came to my career. Business was booming. I had so much confidence in who I was as a businesswoman, a friend, a daughter. But when it came to love, I still hadn't figured out how to walk away from what wasn't working.

I knew this transformation would require a big move— literally.

My lease in the East Village was about to be up. I had always dreamed of living in a luxury high-rise, so I found the best one in Manhattan, made an appointment to see the apartments, and within three days, I was signing a lease on a brand-new, 46th-floor jewel box in the sky that cost way more per month than I should have been spending. But it was exactly what I needed to put some distance between myself and the life I wanted to leave behind.

I moved in on February 2nd. My new place sat between Chinatown and the Lower East Side, tucked into a sleek glass tower with three doormen and a skyline view that stretched for miles. My new backyard was the Manhattan Bridge. I remember unpacking and feeling a wave of calm and safety settle over me.

I bought myself a brand-new bed because no amount of sage could cleanse the energy of the last one. That first night, I lit all of my candles, poured a glass of champagne, and stared out at my new, epic view of the city. I crawled into my fresh new sheets, wrapped myself in the comfort of my next chapter, and made a promise to start fresh, to focus on myself, to finally leave the past behind me.

I was settling into my new life, feeling happy, grounded, and at peace, when the little voice inside my head whispered, *You seem happy. Maybe you should go fuck that all up.*

I had been in my new apartment one full week when I fired off a *Hey stranger* text to Matteo, thinking I had the perfect excuse to reach out. *I moved.*

Two hours later, he replied with a five-minute-long voice note telling me how crazy life had been, how much he missed me, how he needed to see me immediately, how he missed my face and the sound of my voice, how he couldn't stop thinking about me—the works.

We texted nonstop for the next few days. He invited me to a private party he was throwing that Saturday at a new bar he had just opened. I said yes and immediately felt like I was going to throw up—but in a good way.

He called me the morning of the party to confirm and told me again how he couldn't wait to see me. After spending the entire day obsessing over every possible scenario in the group chat, my girlfriends and I had a few different *visions* going. This was my favorite:

I show up alone, looking radiant and sexy in my favorite black leather pants, my black silk Vince blouse that makes me look a good eight to ten pounds skinnier, and perfectly tousled hair. Edgy, yet chic. Matteo spots me the second I walk in, rushes to greet me, plants me at the bar with a glass of champagne, introduces me to all of his friends, then caters to my every need all night. Finally, we go home, have amazing sex, and *start a normal dating life like two functional adults.*

I meditated on this vision, lit one of High Priestess Selene's magical love candles, set the intention, and got ready for my big night.

Unfortunately, the vision did not pan out.

In reality, I showed up to a hot, overcrowded bar filled with people I had never met, scanned the room, and didn't see Matteo anywhere. I asked a few strangers if they'd seen him.

Someone told me he had to run a quick errand and would be back soon. I sent him a text letting him know I had arrived. He did not reply.

Luckily, I spotted a familiar face from the neighborhood and started chatting over a glass of wine. Minutes turned into an hour. I went outside to call him. No answer. My anxiety built with every passing minute. I paced the block, my hands shaking as I stared at my phone, willing it to ring.

I finally decided to call it a night.

I went back inside, grabbed my coat, set a tip down on the bar, and slung my purse over my shoulder. Just as I was about to leave, Matteo came flying through the door.

He beelined to the bar and started stocking it with bottles of wine. He looked overwhelmed, distracted, busy. Before I could get his attention, I noticed the woman he had walked in with. She was statuesque, a good four inches taller than Matteo. She wore a long, pleated metallic silver skirt and a black wide-brimmed hat. Her makeup was flawless, her highlighter glistening in the candlelight, her lips shining like glass. She stood next to me, trying to get the bartender's attention.

I was closer, so I leaned over and offered to order for her. "What do you want, babe?" I asked, because, you know, girl code.

"A prosecco," she said, without ever looking in my direction.

I waved down the bartender.

"John! Can we get a prosecco?"

"I don't know why it's so hard to get a fucking drink in here," she said, to no one in particular. "My boyfriend owns the place."

I froze.

Matteo walked over to me at the exact moment she said it. I leaned my head back and poured the rest of my chardonnay down my throat as fast as humanly possible.

He leaned in for a hug.

"I'm leaving," I said, furious, my face burning red. I grabbed my coat and bolted for the door. Before I could make it halfway down the block, my phone rang.

"Are you out of your fucking mind?" I yelled.

"Why did you leave?!" he asked.

"You invited me here. You were an hour late. And then you walk in with your *girlfriend*!?"

"Cara, please, it's not what you think. We broke up. She's my ex. I didn't invite her here. She just showed up. I swear! Please come back."

I hung up, hailed a cab, and sobbed the entire way home.

The next morning, I woke up to missed calls and texts from him, begging me to forgive him. He called again Monday afternoon. I finally picked up. He swore they were *no longer together*, that she only called him her boyfriend because she was *delusional*.

That made two of us.

He told me how much he respected me and wanted to make it up to me. I agreed to see him, because a tiny, stubborn piece of me still wanted so badly to believe him.

So we made plans for the next day.

Which just so happened to be Valentine's Day.

And that afternoon, he canceled.

CHAPTER SIX

PARIS SYNDROME

It was close to 4 a.m., and the sky was beginning to lighten from jet black to a deep inky blue, the way it does at that time of year when summer is near. Alex and I lay naked in my bed, listening to The Strokes. The only light in the room came from the twinkling buildings stamped into the Manhattan skyline and the flickering glow of an overpriced Le Labo candle, its flame dancing against a framed picture of Marilyn Monroe leaning on my dresser. Half-empty glasses of red wine surrounded us. Alex's head was curled into the crook of my neck.

"We should talk about what this is," he said.

"What do you mean?" I asked.

"This. You know, what we're doing. We should define it," he said, tracing his fingers along my collarbone.

My stomach fluttered. We had only been seeing each other for a few weeks, but things felt… right. He texted me every day.

He planned real dates. We were already sleeping at each other's places. He even assembled my Dyson vacuum cleaner.

Plus, Alex was a lot like me. Newly divorced. The same age. Clearly a relationship person. I liked him. A lot.

I tried to act like I didn't know what was coming next. In my head, I knew we were about to have *The Talk*. I was about to have a new boyfriend.

"I'm not into relationships," he said bluntly.

I sat up, pulling my white linen duvet over my chest. A man's actions had never felt so entirely different from the words coming out of his mouth. I'd dated emotionally unavailable men before. I typically knew what I was getting myself into right away. But Alex wasn't acting like that. He was acting like my *boyfriend*.

"Oh, of course! I mean, yeah, you should really be out there dating other people. You've only been single for two months! I wouldn't want you to rush into anything," I said, my voice bright and unbothered.

"I really, really love spending time with you, though, and I hope we can continue to."

"Sure!" I said, my stomach flutters turning into nausea.

He rolled on top of me and kissed me, pressing his body against mine. "Look at me," he murmured as he slipped inside me. We made love until the sun came up and fell asleep in each other's arms.

I met Alex at my birthday party. My friend Lucien brought

him, thinking it would be good for me to meet someone from my new neighborhood. That Monday, Lucien called and told me to check my Instagram DMs—Alex was trying to reach me.

I opened my messages and found a note from him:

Hey Cara,

We met yesterday at your birthday party. Happy Birthday! Thanks for having me. I'd love to take you out sometime. There's a walking tour I do on Orchard Street. It's basically me talking about all the dumb things I did in my 20s at all the bars in the neighborhood. Everyone loses interest pretty quickly. Including me. Anyway. Wine at the end of the tour. Let me know what you think.

I read the DM a few times, trying to place Alex's face.

We had both moved to the Lower East Side two months earlier, just two blocks apart. He was living alone for the first time after his divorce. I was desperately trying to escape the East Village, hoping a change in scenery would bring me better karma after my own.

The night of my party had been a blur of glowing single-girl energy, the aftermath of the Matteo situation still fresh in my mind. Alex and I had met, but I wasn't thinking about him in a romantic way. I wasn't thinking about him at all.

I scanned his Instagram. Random photos of buildings. Some artwork. A few dog pics. Not a single selfie in sight.

Good sign.

I responded, agreeing to the date, even though I had no idea who he was. But wine sounded good. Someone brand new sounded good. A first date with a *perfect stranger* on the Lower East Side sounded like the perfect birthday gift and the perfect antidote to my heartbreak.

That Wednesday evening, Alex waited for me in the lobby of my building.

"You look great!" he said, looking me up and down, smiling as I fluttered toward him in grey jeans, metallic silver ballet flats, and a black leather moto jacket.

I blushed. "Thanks! So do you!"

I felt instantly at ease as we walked to a natural wine bar on Orchard Street. He was a good six feet, and I loved how small I felt next to him.

"What do you like to drink?" he asked, pulling my barstool out for me.

"I could do a white. Or a rosé."

"Great." He picked up the menu, scanning it quickly. "We'll start with these," he told the bartender. He was confident. Direct. I liked it.

Our conversation flowed easily. We talked about how weird it was to start over after divorce, where we liked to drink wine in the neighborhood, and how much New York had changed since our early twenties.

I have a rule. If I'm not feeling a date, I bail after one drink. But I was feeling it.

Another round. An hour slipped by, feeling like five minutes.

"Should we do one more?" he asked as we drained our glasses.

I nodded, playing it cool, then excused myself to the bathroom. I fired off a quick text to Blair: *I like him!!!!*

When I returned, two new glasses of wine were waiting. We clinked them together.

"Are you hungry?" he asked.

"I could have a little snack."

"Do you like oysters?"

"Love them."

The moment the words left my lips, he flagged down the bartender and ordered a dozen oysters, a side of fries, and two glasses of champagne. My *dream meal.*

This was the *exact* moment of the date—you know that moment—when I decided I was officially into him.

We laughed, leaned in closer, the wine pulling us toward the edge. I knew that one more glass of anything would take us both over.

And just like that, two more glasses of champagne appeared.

We finished them. I checked my phone. "It's after 11… and it's a school night."

"Should I walk you home?"

"I guess so," I said, pouting.

He took my hand. I wrapped my arm inside his.

"Oneeeeee more?" he grinned.

"Yes!"

We walked into 169 Bar and within minutes we were making out at a table in the corner. His lips were soft. His tongue felt perfect.

"You kiss like me," I murmured.

He grabbed the back of my head and pulled me in closer.

We left the bar, holding hands.

Alex followed me through the revolving doors of my apartment building. My doorman smirked knowingly as we floated through the lobby and upstairs.

♡

It was almost June, and Alex and I had been seeing each other for over a month, but it felt like three. He was taking me out on dates multiple times a week. He texted me every single day. We were sleeping at each other's places. Our sex was getting really good. We had inside jokes. We felt connected.

Although he had made it clear early on that he wasn't ready for anything serious, I wanted him to be mine. He *felt* like mine. But he wasn't. He had made *The Rules* clear that night in my bed.

So when he told me he had plans on a Friday or Saturday night, I'd give him little speeches about how he should have fun! get out there!—which were essentially monologues to convince myself that I was fine with him dating other people.

You know, *when you give a man freedom, he realizes he doesn't want it,* I told my girlfriends.

This was my latest made-up revelation, my personal TED Talk to justify why I was still sleeping with a man who was clearly keeping me at arm's length.

Most of the time, I believed it.

But sometimes—like the night he stopped mid-sex, pulled out, and rolled onto the other side of the bed—I knew I was deluding myself.

"What's wrong?" I asked, blinking at him, completely taken aback.

"I don't know. I can't do this. I'm so confused." His head was in his hands.

"Are you serious right now?"

"I have to go. I have an early morning flight tomorrow."

He got dressed faster than I'd ever seen a man move, grabbed his keys, and bolted out of my apartment before I even had a chance to stand up and walk him out.

I sat there, completely naked, wondering what the hell had just happened.

I considered picking up my phone to call him, but I didn't. Instead, I repeated my own delusional mantra: *Give a man freedom and he'll realize he doesn't want it.*

I turned my phone over, stared at the ceiling, and forced myself to sleep.

The next morning, I woke up to missed calls and texts from

Alex. I made an espresso and paced my apartment, trying to decide whether or not I should call him back. I didn't want to be reactive. I didn't want to scream at him. But I was reeling.

I finally called him.

"Hi. I'm so sorry," he blurted out as soon as he answered.

"What the fuck was that?"

"I'm sorry, Cara. I was just stressed out. I knew I had an early morning and I'm leaving town for the weekend. I didn't want to cancel on you last night because I didn't want to let you down. But I should have just stayed in and packed."

"That's bullshit, Alex."

"No, it's not, I swear."

"That can never happen again. Not like that."

"I know. I need to earn back your trust. That was not okay. I'm so sorry, Cara. You are becoming one of the most important people in my life. You bring so much positivity and happiness to me."

I sat with that for a moment. I wanted to believe him.

Later, I called my best friend to vent. "Fuck him. Are you kidding me? He spiraled while he was INSIDE you? Please never speak to that man again," she begged.

I defended him. I told her people are crazy after a divorce. I recounted my own unhinged behavior. I told myself we'd get through this. I just needed to be patient. I just needed to be cool.

Alex went away for the weekend, texting me constantly, sending photos, checking in. On Monday, we met at a bar near our apartments to talk.

"Cara, again, I'm so sorry about the other night. Are you okay? I feel terrible and I want you to know how much you mean to me. I don't want to lose this," he told me over two glasses of happy hour chenin blanc.

"I don't want to lose this either, Alex. But you can't have your little breakdowns in front of me. Or inside me. And I don't want to be with someone who's confused about me. Maybe you should go to therapy."

"I'm not confused. I swear. That will never happen again."

Alex was reassuring and genuine. He had an honesty about him that I trusted, even when it wasn't what I *wanted* to hear. Fucking Capricorns. This time, I wanted to hear it. I basked in the comfort of his regret for a moment and blocked out the fact that he was leaving for a month.

He had planned a solo escape through France and Italy for the summer. A post-divorce pilgrimage. An attempt to clear his head, to figure out who he was without anyone else's influence.

I told myself it was a good thing. That this space would make him realize he missed me, that he'd go off and be free and come back wanting me more than ever. But deep down, I knew better.

I was haunted.

Haunted by the idea of him fucking hot French girls in hotel rooms with balconies overlooking the Seine.

Haunted by the way he told me he *wasn't into relationships* while holding my face in his hands and fucking me like he was in love with me.

Haunted by that night he ran out of my apartment, his voice shaking, his body stiff with panic, like being with me had felt too real.

We left the bar and I walked him to his apartment. The city was thick with late-spring humidity. The evening air felt heavy and charged. We stood on the sidewalk outside his doorway, the sun dipping low into the golden sky.

"I'll see you in a few weeks," he said, his hands around my waist, pulling me closer.

"Have fun. I'll miss you," I said, squinting up at him against the sunset.

"I'll miss you too." He took my face in both hands and kissed me. This time, he *really* kissed me.

I pulled away after a few moments, squeezed his hand, and walked down the block toward my place.

Three days later, he flew to Paris.

Dear Diary,

Everyone hates you including my psychic. But I always defend you. It's getting harder to do that.

I send you a poem at 7:29 am that I found on the internet. I think I am still drunk from the night before. But I would have sent it regardless.

I go on a date while you are away with a guy who wears a single hoop earring and tells me my lips feel like pillows. I come home and text you back from my bed.

I'm so tired of counting six hours ahead and wondering whether you're having coffee or wine or fucking some French bitch or maybe an Italian one.

Remember when you told me you loved the way I kissed you? "So complete," you said while you were fucking me.

You haven't texted me in five days which means you're most likely on a bender and dealing with your ex-wife – good luck!!! I hope you never text me again so I don't have to decide whether or not I'm responding to you.

I read once that if you feel down you can force yourself to smile and it will put you in a better mood.

CHAPTER SEVEN

MY VERY BEAUTIFUL FRIEND

The Saturday Alex returned from Europe, I deep-cleaned my apartment all day, showered, got ready, and told everyone I was busy.

Just in case.

We had no solid plans to see each other when he got back. In fact, I wasn't even sure he was coming back that day, but I did some girl math based on his texts, his radio silence on Instagram, and the general rhythm of his disappearances. I assumed he was on a plane.

At 4:30 p.m., my phone rang. It was him.

My heart pounded as I cleared my throat and let it ring twice—three times—before answering. I didn't want to sound like I'd been waiting all day, obsessing over the timeline of his return like a desperate, delusional non-girlfriend.

"Hello?" I said, masking my excitement.

"Hey! How are you?" His voice was flat and familiar, like

nothing had changed.

"I'm great. Welcome back!"

"Thanks! Yeah sooo... I just got back from the airport and realized I lost my keys and can't get into my apartment."

"Oh no. Wanna come here?"

I had never been happier about someone else's shit luck.

"Yeah, would that be okay?"

"Of course! See you in a few."

I hung up and ran to the bathroom, touching up my makeup like my life depended on it. Alex lived five minutes away so I didn't have much time. I spritzed my Le Labo perfume behind my ears, ran a brush through my hair, and darted to the door just as my buzzer rang.

Alex stood in front of me, grinning like a Cheshire cat, his cheeks flushed, his hair wild, his green cargo pants covered in stains. He reeked of alcohol.

He was a mess.

Still, I thought he looked beautiful.

He wrapped me in a tight hug.

"I missed you," I said.

"Missed you too," he murmured against my forehead.

Alex dropped his backpack onto the floor, then pulled a black plastic grocery bag onto my counter, digging inside. He pulled out a six-pack of Peroni.

"Want one?" he asked, already cracking open a sweaty bottle.

"No thanks, I have champagne."

We chatted about his flight, his Airbnb roommates (all women, apparently, which I tried not to react to), and the places he'd been.

And then, just as quickly as he'd arrived, he stood up.

"Okay, I'm gonna go meet Brandon for a drink."

My stomach dropped.

"Oh. Okay. Sure."

"I won't be long. Maybe like an hour or two tops? Then we can meet back up and go get some dinner or something?"

"Totally. I have plans with Lucien anyway."

I did not have plans with Lucien. But I was about to make them.

"Sounds good." He pulled me close, kissing me deep and slow, and for a moment, I forgot how much this felt like being on a leash.

"See you in a little bit."

Forty-five minutes later, just as I had arrived at some birthday party I was now crashing, I got a text from Alex: Done with Brandon. Meet at Le Dive?

I kissed Lucien hello and goodbye in the same breath, turned on my heel, and slid right back into an Uber.

♡

Alex and I were still seeing each other by the end of summer. As we grew closer, as we spent more and more nights together, he made it clearer and clearer that we were never going to be serious.

One night, he invited me over to cook dinner at his place. The candles I suggested he buy flickered in the kitchen. He handed me a glass of wine. The atmosphere was warm, intimate, *couple-y*.

"Hey, wanna stop off at my friend's art gallery before we eat? I want you to meet him."

"Sure!"

We finished our drinks, walked a few blocks, and entered the gallery.

"Tim! I want you to meet my friend, Cara."

I felt my entire body go numb.

On the way home, I was quiet. But by the time we got back to his place, I couldn't hold it in anymore.

"Why did you introduce me as your friend?" I asked, leaning against the kitchen island.

Alex pulled a bottle of white wine out of the fridge. His fridge always had white wine.

"Because you are," he said, so matter-of-factly, it felt like a punch.

"So we're not dating?"

"You know I hate those terms." He shrugged. "You're my very beautiful friend."

"Oh okay. So do you have sex with all your friends?"

"Not all of them." He laughed.

He pulled me into a hug. I tried to push him away.

"I'm serious, Alex. We are not friends."

He kissed my cheek. I melted into him.

♡

Alex and I drank a lot together—too much.

We spent every weekend drunk, from the moment we met up until the moment we passed out.

"Are you guys on another bender?" my friend Tara texted when I ignored her for three days.

Alex and I tried meeting for coffee once. After we finished our coffees, we went straight to a bar across the street and drank for two days.

One weekend, he booked us a room at a cheap budget hotel in Chinatown for no reason.

"Tiffany and Chad, here for our engagement weekend!" I announced to the front desk.

We drank champagne out of paper cups in the hotel's sad excuse for a lobby bar, then went upstairs and had sex with all the lights on.

We spent 48 hours locked in that room, fucking, drinking, drawing fake tattoos on each other with a Sharpie.

"This is how rich kids wind up in rehab," my friend Tara told me when I called her the next day.

♡

Drinking with Alex was a wildcard. It dulled the pain of knowing he'd never be mine. It silenced the part of me that wanted to scream every time he flirted with someone else.

It made us hornier, more uninhibited, more reckless.

"You are so gorgeous. Imagine if you lost, like, twenty pounds?" he said one night, mid-champagne buzz.

I got up and locked myself in the bathroom.

"Cara, come back! I'm kidding," he laughed.

I stared at myself in the mirror. I looked so drunk.

What are you doing with this man?

I came out of the bathroom a few minutes later and slunk back onto the living room floor with him. He kissed me passionately and we made love, right there, on the ground.

Dear Diary,

I ride the elevator in my new luxury apartment building braless in oversized mismatched pajamas and broken flip flops downstairs to pick up my keto ice cream delivery. Is this confidence or is this giving up?

I tell myself I'll stay in. Go to bed early. I buy those Zzzquil gummies that Blair recommends but I just don't see myself as the kind of person who takes sleep aids. So instead I meet friends out at the tail end of their day drinking adventures and have a few glasses of wine with them and come home and go to sleep alone. That's getting real boring.

I remember when you sent me a postcard from your trip to Europe and I thought it was really romantic and you said, "Yeah I bought a bunch of them and sent them out to people."

I sometimes wonder if I will ever be in a real relationship again.

It seems like the thing that always came so naturally to me now feels like the most impossible feat.

But so many ugly people are in love. It's weird.

CHAPTER EIGHT

TO LIVE AND DATE IN LA

"**I** have a date Thursday," I say casually, stretching in bed next to Alex on a Sunday morning.

"That's great," he says, completely unfazed. "You should go. Have fun."

There is no hesitation. No flicker of jealousy. Not even a single question. No *What kind of guy? Where'd you meet him?* Nothing.

The date is with an older guy, a friend of a friend, who looks like Blake Shelton but fatter. I don't want to go, but I'm forcing myself, mostly because I want to see if Alex will react. He doesn't.

I decide I need more dates. I get back on the apps that Monday morning as if I am clocking in for a job. I begin aggressively swiping on men. Paying Hinge $19.99 to boost my profile so more people can view it. I'm hoping being around other men somehow changes my energy.

The universe intervenes in the form of a gig. My friend Blair is hosting a women's empowerment brunch in Los Angeles and invites me to speak on a panel. I say yes immediately. A trip is exactly what I need. Sunshine, blue skies, and most importantly, a solid distraction.

The first night in LA, Blair and I are drinking at our hotel bar when a 6'2 investment banker named AJ strikes up a conversation. He wears a Rolex and smells like fresh laundry. Blair, in full wing-woman mode, invites him to dinner with us. I nod and smile but spend the entire meal checking my phone, waiting for a text from Alex.

After dinner, we get in the elevator. Blair gets off on the sixth floor, leaving AJ and me to ride up to eight. "Are we saying goodnight already?" he asks.

I smile. "Follow me."

Inside my room, I face the wall to change into pajamas while commanding him to open the mini-bar champagne. "The *Vanderpump Rules* finale is coming on right now. We *have* to watch."

AJ pours two glasses and sits stiffly on the bed, waiting.

"We're not hooking up, just so you know," I tell him as I slide under the covers. "But you can cuddle me."

He wraps an arm around me, and I fall asleep in ten minutes. An hour later, I wake up just enough to feel him gently pull away, kiss me on the forehead, and leave.

I never see him again.

The next morning, I decide I love Los Angeles.

I love how far away it is from my life. I convince myself that being bicoastal is the answer. Before my flight home, I set my Bumble location to LA, a trick I learned from a friend who likes dating men in cities she has no intention of moving to.

Within minutes, I match with Max, a cute tattooed chef with a dad bod and a spatula inked on his forearm. He messages first.

○ **Him:** "Do you live in LA?"

○ **Me:** "I'm based in New York, but I go back and forth all the time," I lie.

○ **Him:** "Oh, nice. When are you here next?"

○ **Me:** "In a few weeks!" I lie again.

I have no plans to be there in a few weeks, but I will make them.

Max and I text nonstop for the next two weeks. We never speak on the phone, but I don't mind. He tells me he wants something serious, that he's looking for *his person*. We start calling each other babe. We sext.

It feels like something.

I call my friend Jenna, who lives in LA, and tell her I need to come visit. We pick a date, two weeks out. I tell Max I'm coming back. My flight is booked. The plan is to spend a few days with Jenna, then the weekend at Max's place in Echo Park. Still, I have never heard his voice.

On the flight to LA, Max and I text the entire time. "Baby,

I can't wait to see you. I can't believe you're almost here!"

I send a sexy window seat selfie. "I know, babe. So close."

When I land, he greets me at baggage claim with a hug. He is 5'6, not 5'10 as he described in his dating profile. All men on the dating apps inflate their height by at least three inches. It's science. He grabs my luggage, leads me to the elevator, and lunges at my face with his entire tongue. I am slightly plane-drunk, so I go along with it.

We go for tacos and margaritas, then back to my hotel. We have sex. It's fine. We wake up and do it again. He leaves to get coffee, kisses me on the cheek, and then barely texts me for the next two days.

By Thursday, we're sitting on my patio, drinking wine before heading to his place. Max talks nonstop. How his career is failing. How he can't pay his mortgage. How his ex was a bipolar alcoholic who cheated on him. I am now aggressively drinking my chardonnay, attempting to coach him out of his bad mood and attempting to get myself into a better one.

I offer him an out. "Hey, I can totally just stay with Jenna this weekend if you need time to yourself!"

"Are you nuts? I'm dying to spend the weekend with you," he says, making zero eye contact. I ignore the sinking feeling in my gut.

Max is a perfect host. There's a new toothbrush waiting for me in his bathroom. The thermostat is constantly set to 68 so I won't overheat. A bottle of Pellegrino is always in my reach.

We sleep in the same bed. We never have sex again.

By Friday night, the news warns of an unprecedented hurricane hitting LA. "This is going to be BAD," Max says, staring at the TV. I secretly change my flight to the next morning.

"Should I leave early?" I ask, feigning concern.

"Yeah, I mean, I'd love to spend more time with you, but I don't want you to get trapped here." Too late.

The next morning, Max drops me at LAX. We say goodbye. He hugs me. It's the first time he has touched me in two days.

I walk into the Delta lounge, take out my phone, and fire off a text to Alex: "Fuck LA."

Dear Diary,

Everything I love gets discontinued, dies, or is emotionally unavailable.

Isn't it wild how most relationships fail, yet it's like we have amnesia every time and we just do it over and over again? Sometimes dating just feels like calling a new stranger "babe" every couple of months.

Have you ever completely repelled another human being simply by being yourself? Fortunately, Instagram scripture tells me rejection is projection and I do agree but it's just so weird when someone suddenly starts acting like your coworker from the accounting department after you've seen their penis?

I once told a stranger on a first date the names I have picked out for the children I don't ever plan on having and I think that is more intimate than sex.

I wonder if everyone on that flight from LAX to JFK knew that I was having a mental breakdown in seat 8D? I cried so hard I had to excuse myself from the Delta One cabin and go into the bathroom and cry harder. I kept my airpods in with my Sad Girl After Hours playlist bumpin' for dramatic effect while I watched myself cry in the mirror to Fiona Apple. I definitely felt like I was in a movie. Don't we all feel like that sometimes? I came out and discovered a fresh glass of white wine at my seat. LOL.

I wake up with a horrible nagging feeling that I ruined everything by being myself.

CHAPTER NINE

LOVE LETTERS

I t was autumn in New York and my love life was falling apart just as quickly as the leaves fell from the trees. I was channeling my pain (and my cringe) into my writing. But I didn't stop there. I'd started taking my stories to the stage; baring it all in front of live audiences.

My writing coach, Chloe, connected me with the producer of *Generation Women*, one of New York's major monthly storytelling shows. I threw my name in the ring and somehow I landed a spot. From the moment I hit the stage and shared my words with a live audience, I was hooked. There was nothing else I wanted to do.

Then one brisk Sunday morning as I nursed a brutal hangover from staying up too late with Alex or agonizing over whether or not he was out with someone else (I can't quite remember), I got an email.

Happy Sunday, Cara—

Georgia recommended you for my storytelling show: *Love Letters! - True Stories of First Love, Last Love, & All The Love In Between*. *Love Letters* is a one-day off-Broadway show in NYC. The in-person show auditions are at Jude Moore studios.

I read the email twice, squealed, and then immediately screen shotted it and fired it off to everyone in my phone who I knew would be just as excited as I was. Something about this opportunity felt huge—like *life-changing* huge.

I clicked the calendar link in the email and locked down my in-person audition. I had three weeks to get it together. I'd have to pick the perfect essay, polish it up, and rehearse it until I could do it in my sleep. I landed on a piece about my early childhood dream of being a fabulous, single, independent, rich divorcee. This fantasy of mine—of being a glamorous, man-hating, ex-wife—had taken quite a detour by the time I actually reached my goal of getting divorced in 2020.

The essay came with a twist. Turns out, post-divorce, I was more in love *with love* than ever before. It was funny, brutally honest, and raw—the perfect fit for the show, and a mirror of where I was in life, even though real love was nowhere to be found.

The three weeks leading up to the audition flew by. I was excited, nervous, and completely preoccupied. My head was spinning with thoughts of Alex and the seven-month roller-coaster ride I couldn't seem to get off. I tried to set boundaries,

I tried to walk away, but the truth was painfully clear: I was all talk and no action.

Then things got even worse. Three days before my audition for *Love Letters*, Alex's ex-wife crashed a women's empowerment panel I was speaking on. She showed up alone, no ticket, just standing there, lurking in the corner, watching me like a bad actress in a Lifetime movie.

I held it together flawlessly, because, well, #professionalism. But inside, I was trembling, sick to my stomach, and trying not to picture her raising her hand mid-panel to scream at me for fucking her ex-husband. Why was she there? What had Alex been telling her to provoke this? Was she really that bold, or was I suddenly a new cast member on *The Real Housewives of the Lower East Side*?

Two nights later, I found myself sitting across from Alex at a bar. I can't explain why I went. I can't explain why I hadn't ended this mess months ago. I can't explain why I was still putting up with all this bullshit.

"Cara, I'm really sorry again about what happened," he said, apologizing for his ex's antics.

"Oh, it's fine," I replied with a smirk. "I mean, you could have sent me flowers to make up for it, but you're not that type of guy." Alex had declared back when we started dating that he thought flowers were "cliché."

"I'd send you flowers if I liked you enough."

For a second, I was frozen. Then I grabbed my purse and

walked out without a word. Alex ran after me, chasing me down Orchard Street.

"Fuck off!" I yelled, picking up my pace as he ran beside me, grabbing my arm to slow me down. How that block had changed for us.

"Cara, I'm sorry! I didn't mean it," he pleaded.

"Don't fucking touch me, Alex! I'm done!"

I started to jog and he ran beside me, following me for five blocks. Finally, we reached a corner where the walk sign turned red, trapping us together while traffic rushed by. He dropped to the sidewalk, his hands folded in a prayer pose, begging me to forgive him.

"I was kidding!" he insisted.

"You're pathetic," I shot back, rolling my eyes as he took my hand.

Alex was always kidding, always sorry—whenever he let his real feelings slip and I reacted. The same movie on repeat.

We walked on through the brisk autumn night toward the Manhattan Bridge, the wind cutting across our faces. When we reached my apartment, he trailed behind me through the revolving doors and up the stairs, as if nothing had happened.

I woke up the next morning with a raging hangover, the bright Saturday sun blazing through my floor-to-ceiling windows. My eyes burned, my throat felt like sandpaper, and with barely three hours of sleep, I squinted at my phone. It was almost 11 a.m.

"You need to leave. My audition's at 12:30," I muttered, nudging Alex awake.

We'd spent the night talking, drinking, fucking, and doing everything but making amends. Alex tossed out a few half-hearted apologies, hoping I'd get drunk enough to forgive him. I pretended to let it slide but I didn't. Out of all his stunts, this one stung the most. Or maybe, finally, I'd hit my breaking point. Seven months of trying to fix him, only to realize he was unfixable. And the only one broken was me.

I threw on my black silk robe and dragged myself to the kitchen for a double espresso, cursing myself for letting him stay over the night before one of the biggest days of my career. Alex stumbled out and gave me a quick hug as he laced up his shoes.

"Good luck today. You'll kill it," he said, heading out the door. I didn't even answer.

As soon as he was gone, I checked my Uber app. Twenty minutes to the studio. I downed my coffee, jumped into the shower. There was no time to wash my hair, so I felt even grosser. I slapped on some tinted moisturizer, concealer, and eyeliner, picked up yesterday's outfit off the floor and threw it on, and ordered my car. Praying I didn't smell like Alex and white wine, I grabbed my purse and dashed out.

The second we hit the FDR, traffic was at a standstill. My leg started bouncing. Minutes slipped by, and soon it was past noon. I fired off an apologetic email to the producer, letting her know I was running late. This was *not* me. I'm the girl who's thirty minutes early. The one who considers herself late when she's on time. The girl who doesn't screw up jobs.

"I'm running so late. This is awful!" I texted Alex.

No response.

By the time I reached Jude Moore Studios, it was 1:15 p.m. My heart pounded as I stepped out of the car, forty-five minutes late. I spotted the sign: *Love Letters auditions, 4th floor*. I flew up the stairs, desperately trying to catch my breath and pull myself together.

When I reached the fourth floor, sweating and gasping, I swung open the door and launched into an apology, only to realize I'd interrupted another audition. *Great.*

"Hi, Cara. We'll be with you in a few minutes. You can wait outside," the producer said sharply.

I wanted to disappear. Late and rude. I considered running out of there, going back to my bed to hide and erase this whole mess from my mind. I checked my phone. Alex still hadn't answered.

CHAPTER TEN

HAPPY NEW YEAR

I've been thinking about what I want to tell you next. I could detail December, and tell you that Alex and I spent Christmas together. I could tell you that I got him a thoughtful present but was too embarrassed to give it to him when he showed up empty-handed at my apartment that day.

I could tell you that we also spent New Year's Eve together. I could tell you that he paraded me around the city all night, proudly introducing me to his friends, holding my hand with the care and affection of a loving partner. I could tell you that despite how affectionate and adoring he was that night, I still found him outside the party we were at, smoking cigarettes with a model half my age.

I could tell you that we woke up on New Year's Day and he said to me, *Maybe I should just be your boyfriend?*

I could also tell you that the year had been so toxic for me that I decided to move back to the East Village. The beautiful,

46th floor luxury apartment I dubbed my "jewel box in the sky" had become a representation of the chaos I had invited into my life and continued to entertain—one sleepless, drunken night after the next with a man who was now becoming dangerous to me. I had to go.

You haven't been yourself in a long time. My friend's words rang in my mind as I bubble wrapped my life. Again. My move was scheduled for January 2. Fresh start. Brand new year. Moving. Again. I always arranged my leases like that.

Alex came with me on New Year's Day to pick up my keys. *I can't believe you're doing this,* he said over and over again that day. *I can't believe you're leaving.*

He begged me to come back to his place that night. I reluctantly agreed even though I knew I still had so much to do before the morning. He made us salmon for dinner. I eyed the packaging. *Farmed.* Noted.

We had sex and afterward I got up and started getting dressed. He grabbed my arm and pulled me back into bed, pleading with me to stay over. I refused and finished pulling my sweater over my head.

The next morning I relocated my belongings—and my sanity—two miles north.

I had been in my new apartment for only a few days when Alex called me at 11 p.m. one night asking if he could come over. He stumbled in, the stench of wine entering my space before he did, and sank into my couch with the casualness of someone who had no idea he was about to break me for the last time. Through his slurry drunken laughter, he confessed he had been dating someone else for the past month.

At first I thought he was joking, but I quickly realized he was dead serious.

When? I asked him over and over again. *When?* We were together constantly. *When* had he penciled in a brand new girlfriend? *When?*

He passed out in my bed an hour later. I had no real answers from him but I had one very clear answer from myself—I was done. I had reached my end.

$\heartsuit$

Alex let me go without any of the fanfare I tried to keep him with for all those months. Untangling myself from him was easy. In one seven-minute phone call, he apologized for hurting me, mentioned he left the other woman, and I told him it was too late. That was it. No fighting for me, no begging—just a quiet, *I understand* from him. *Call ended.*

And honestly? I wasn't even sad. I was relieved. I felt like I finally had a reason to go, although anyone else in their right mind would have identified a million reasons to walk away much earlier than I did.

But the change in scenery was helping. The new year was helping. And the new play I was in was about to become center stage in my life. Somehow, the audition I was convinced I'd bombed landed me a role in *Love Letters*.

It felt like a new chapter, a fresh start. Like everything was finally falling into place. But I didn't know then that the biggest plot twist was still ahead.

CHAPTER ELEVEN

LOVE LESSONS

"All that matters is that you spare yourself nothing and wear yourself out and risk everything to find something that seems true." —TONY KUSHNER

J ackson arrived like a hurricane—fast, disruptive, and impossible to ignore.

We met in the cast of *Love Letters*, rehearsing on Zoom from opposite ends of the country. I was in New York City, living my loud, ambitious, creatively chaotic life, and he was somewhere sunny where the air smelled like sea salt and suburbia. Where weekends were spent running kids around town to soccer games and friends' houses, not in dive bars but in drive-thrus and school parking lots, in backyards strung with bistro lights, where the biggest thrill was a new restaurant opening at the mall.

His world moved slower, steadier. Mine was electric and unpredictable. I lived for the buzz of a crowded coffee shop and graffiti-painted walls, the hum of taxis at 2 a.m., the rush of an idea hitting me mid-sip of my morning espresso in my East Village apartment. He lived for routine, for comfort, for early bedtimes and quiet weekend mornings with his daughters. We were opposites in every possible way.

But somehow, he felt like home.

The first time I heard him introduce himself on that Zoom meeting, it was like recognizing someone I had known my whole life. There were about twenty of us on that call, but he was the only one I heard. He spoke about the bands he grew up listening to—Taking Back Sunday, The Get Up Kids, Rancid, The Bouncing Souls, and Blink-182—all the same ones I loved—and how he thrived on living life on his own terms; rebelliously and with passion. And when he went back on mute after his introduction, he kept his camera on, folding laundry like he had no idea I was watching him from my own little square. I searched the chat for his Instagram handle, found it, followed him immediately, and five minutes later, a DM from him popped up.

We exchanged phone numbers that evening, and within hours, we were texting nonstop, our voices filling the spaces between messages on three-hour phone calls, stretching long into the night like we had known each other forever. A few days later, he suggested a FaceTime date. We'd cook dinner together, salmon, rice, and veggies, in our respective kitchens.

I propped my phone up against my toaster, laughing as it kept slipping, while he teased me about my lack of a tripod. The next morning, a package arrived at my door. Inside was a tripod, neatly wrapped, with a note that read: *You're gonna need this.*

Within two weeks of that first Zoom call, he was on a plane to see me.

The minute I opened my door and saw him standing there, we locked eyes and leapt into each other's arms, holding on so tightly I could feel the heat of his body through my clothes, the smell of his skin so familiar as I buried my face into his shoulder. I had never missed someone I had only just met, but that was exactly how it felt. And then, we kissed. Instantly. Without hesitation. It was desperate and certain, the kind of first kiss that screams, *this. This is it.* And although I never believed in love at first sight, this was as close as I had ever come.

Our first date lasted three days and we barely left my apartment. We stayed up late listening to music we both loved, laughing loudly, eating candy and caviar, drinking wine and trading stories of our teenage years, where we lived strangely parallel lives. We were both divorced, and we both spoke candidly of our pasts, sharing the same hope for the future.

By the time he left, we were in deep.

I always said my two non-negotiables in relationships were dating a man with children and dating long-distance. I was obsessed with my freedom, with the life I had built—one where nothing and no one could slow me down. If you weren't down for a spontaneous weekend getaway to Mexico, I didn't see how things could work. If you had to cancel a date to stay home with a sick kid, I was not interested. Give me bougie late-night dinners—not school pick-up lines.

Yet here I was, falling in love with a man who made me question both. I didn't care. I had finally met the man I had been searching for in everyone else. He felt like my best friend. My twin flame.

Soon after our three-day first date and an impromptu trip to visit him, I met his parents and his daughters at our *Love Letters* performance in New York. That afternoon, over sushi, I fell in love with his girls. They were extensions of him—the same quick wit, the same expressive eyes, the same unfiltered enthusiasm when talking about the things they loved. I tried to play it cool, but I was in awe, watching the way they looked up to him, how easily they teased him, how naturally they let me into their orbit.

It felt like we had known each other for a lifetime.

We dove headfirst into our relationship, and even though the universe had thrown me the ultimate curveball, one I never saw coming, I was loving every single second of it.

He'd send me heartfelt texts every day that we jokingly called wedding vows because they were that intense.

○ **Him:** Cara... you are everything to me. You are inspiration. You are hope. You are freedom. You are bliss. You are a world I was afraid I would never see.

💬 **Me:** I keep waiting to wake up from the best dream ever.

💬 **Him:** When you do, there will be three girls thanking you for showing them what a woman can be. And a man next to you saying 'I hope you slept well, my love. Let me make you some coffee.'

It wasn't just how he made me feel—seen, adored, like I was the rarest jewel he'd ever found. It was how he was with them. The softness in his voice when he talked to his girls, the way he made them feel safe and protected in a world that had already shifted under their feet. I thought: *This is the kind of father I'd want for my own children. The kind of man I'd trust with my whole heart.*

I found myself on a flight every seven days or so, coming down to see him. I didn't mind the travel at all—in fact, it was a breath of fresh air and a welcome respite from bustling New York City. His home started to feel more familiar than my own. Soon I was helping him decorate, ordering pink bath towels from Target for me and his daughters, replacing the old beach towels in his linen closet. I stocked his fridge with fancy cheeses and got us new bedding. We hung drapes throughout the place and made sure we always had fresh flowers on the table. I had candles lit all the time.

"You made this place feel like a home," he'd tell me over and over.

I loved our life. I loved our long mid-week lunches followed by record shopping. I loved drinking wine with him on the water at sunset. Laughing for hours, watching *Love Is Blind*, eating snacks in bed.

I loved having mind-blowing sex, and making love for the very first time in my life.

I loved the way he looked into my eyes while we made love and whispered, *let's make a baby.*

We had an intimacy I never knew was possible. I was suddenly rethinking everything I thought I knew about myself. We talked about a future—a real future. We talked about rings. Living situations. All of it.

Everyone in my life was thrilled for me. "You literally manifested this man!" one of my best friends said to me one morning. And I truly felt like I did.

The sheer thrill I felt being in his presence, coupled with the comfort of being wholly, fully loved, was a feeling like no other on this earth. I felt safe. I felt prioritized. I felt valued. I felt adored.

I was head over heels in love.

One Tuesday afternoon, as I sat at his kitchen table talking about school with his youngest daughter, waiting for his parents to join us for dinner, my phone buzzed.

It was an email from a woman who worked for him.

Subject: *Just a note.*
"Cara, I'm not even sure where to start. I don't even know if you will see this, but I need to make some things clear about Jackson..."

My heart felt like it stopped beating. I continued reading the most devastating email a woman desperately in love with a man she believed was her soulmate could read. The words blurred together. I couldn't hear a thing anymore—not his daughter's voice beside me, not the sound of the wind chimes outside the window. My hands trembled as I scrolled.

Just a note.

The kind of note that rewires your entire existence in an instant. The kind of note that turns love into a lie before you've even had a chance to process what it means. I told myself to breathe, told myself not to show it on my face, because his parents were about to walk through the door. Because the house smelled like fresh sauce for the pasta we were making. Because we were with his kids. Because I wasn't ready for this world to collapse just yet.

"Jackson, can we go for a walk?" I said, my voice shaking.

"Of course, babe," he said.

We got a few feet away from the house before I handed him my phone, the email opened.

"What the fuck is this?" I asked, catching my breath, my stomach twisting and turning.

He scanned the email, his face flickering between confusion and guilt.

"Cara, let me explain."

"What is there to explain? Is this all true?"

We stood in the Publix parking lot as I questioned him

like a cop uncovering a crime. His hands shook as he tried to talk his way through it. But at that moment, it didn't even matter what his answers were.

I *knew*.

Jackson hadn't cheated on me. I almost wished it were that black and white. It was more complicated than that.

He had spent years collecting women's attention like currency, leaving a trail of broken hearts behind him.

And now, those women had found me.

And my inbox had become their hotline.

I didn't tell a soul about the email. Or the DMs that followed. I was in the middle of a two-week trip visiting him, and I tried my best to block it all out. Jackson had done a good job convincing me that he had, in fact, *changed*. That it was all, in fact, *in the past*.

I believed him. I was desperate to.

♡

We were scheduled to fly back to New York together, just in time for my birthday. Two nights before our trip, I lay in bed, staring at the ceiling. Sleep wouldn't come. My body was buzzing and not with excitement, not with love, but with something darker. It felt like a warning.

Am I making a huge mistake?

Sure, people make bad choices. Sure, this was all in his past. He swore I had given him a reason to be a better man, and all I wanted was to believe him. I *needed* to believe him. People could change. I had seen it firsthand. *I was a life coach, for God's sake—I built my career on the belief that people could change.*

Surely, Jackson could change, too.

But that night, sleep never came. I reached for my phone, the room completely silent except for the sound of the ceiling fan and his steady breath beside me. It was 2 a.m. I unlocked my screen and opened my DMs.

Another message.

Another woman.

Another story.

The sun came up, but I never closed my eyes. I felt outside of myself, like I was watching my life play out on a screen. Jackson made coffee, kissed my forehead, went about his morning, completely unaware that something had cracked open inside me. I could barely look at him.

I told him I needed some space. That I wanted to be alone for a bit. Then I grabbed my bag, walked out the door, and didn't stop moving until I found a bar.

It wasn't even noon. I didn't care. I ordered a glass of white wine and called my mom.

"I have something to tell you," I said, my voice cracking.

"What happened? Are you okay?"

"I'm fine," I lied. "But I need to show you something."

I forwarded her the email.

I could hear her scrolling in silence.

Two minutes later, her voice cut through the line like a knife.

"Cara. *Come home.*"

That was all it took.

I booked the first flight out for the next morning.

Dear Diary,

I hate that I miss you. I hate that I think about your kids every day. I hate that I couldn't have just stayed in a bubble and ignored it all.

I listened to our playlists all day yesterday. I'd give anything to go back to that time before I knew better. You ruined a lot of songs for me.

I spent the day in bed. I drank two pots of French press coffee and sent voice memos to friends. I want you to text me but I also don't.

How can I miss someone who wasn't real? How can I miss a man who lied to my face? Was any of it real? This is what haunts me every day.

Was any of it real?

The day we got our matching tattoos is on loop in my brain. God I was so sure of you. People keep asking me if I'll cover it up. I don't want to. Isn't that sad? Some days it's a reminder of the rarest love I've ever felt. Some days it's a reminder of how broken you were. I'll wear both of those things forever now.

I can't hear your voice. I can't hear you say baby.

I want to tell you everything all the time. I wonder if you're going to mail back my clothes. I think about all the things I got for your house. Do you think about me when you lay in those new sheets? Do you still light those candles at night? Did the people at the wine bar ask what happened to me? What did you tell them?

CHAPTER TWELVE

THE SPACE BETWEEN

I was back in New York. Jackson and I weren't speaking. I was taking space, trying to process the whirlwind that had come in like yet another hurricane—just like he did—turning my world upside down.

I gave my number to a few of the women Jackson had fucked over before he met me. I wanted them to call me. I needed to hear their voices, needed to know if they saw the same man I did.

They did not.

Their stories spilled through the phone, identical in all the worst ways. Each one a slight variation of the next— love-bombing, grand gestures, promises whispered late at night, followed by disrespect, distance, and betrayal. It turned out my Prince Charming was, in fact, the ultimate fuck boy.

I listened in disgust. I listened in fascination. I listened because I needed to believe it. To reinforce what I already knew, to push myself further away from him. Or maybe, if I'm being honest, I listened to hurt myself a little more.

Because if I could convince myself he wasn't real, then maybe I could walk away before I got in even deeper.

Because deep down, I *did* know this was real.

And that was the scariest part.

What if this love was everything I had ever wanted, and I lost it anyway? What if I got even more attached, even more invested, and it shattered later—when the stakes were even higher? What if this was the love that could ruin me?

Maybe it was easier to run now than to risk the inevitable. Maybe it was easier to sabotage something before it had the chance to break me completely.

Because this love felt bigger than me. And I wasn't sure I was ready for it.

And yet, in between the horror stories from those women before me, I found myself flooded with memories of *us*. The way he looked at me the first night we spent together. The way he'd pat his chest in bed, wordlessly inviting me to lay on him, whispering that I was the love of his life. The way he made me feel so seen.

I reminded myself: He never did any of that to me. These were *their* stories. They didn't have to be *my* truth.

People grow, right? People learn from their mistakes. People do better...don't they?

I listened to the playlists he made me, trying to mentally time-travel back to when things felt pure and unvarnished.

Before my world crumbled. Even if it was a fantasy land, I craved any relief from the hell I was now living in.

My birthday came and went. I partied with a few friends that weekend and came home feeling empty. I went to psychics for guidance. Watched countless tarot readings on YouTube for answers.

Still, I felt haunted. Part of me wanted to get on a flight, crawl back into his bed, and pretend none of this had happened.

Another part of me wanted to call him and scream, to drag every last lie out of him, to make him *feel* the hurt the way I was feeling it.

But in the end, I didn't do either of those things. I picked up my phone and did the hardest thing imaginable.

I let him go.

💬 **Me:** I have thought long and hard about all of this. I am at my end. I can't shake this feeling. It's affecting my sanity. It's affecting my work. I wish I didn't have to know any of this. I wish we could go back, but we can't. I have to walk away. I hope you understand.

💬 **Him:** I gave everything I had to us. I hope you know that you showed me love like I had never known. I will love you eternally, Cara.

That was it.

No fight. No grand gesture. No desperate plea to stay.

Just two text bubbles. A goodbye far too small for what we were.

And somehow, that made it worse.

I cried for days. I wondered if I had ruined the best thing that had ever happened to me.

Because the cruelest thing about breaking up with someone you're still in love with is that, for a while, it doesn't feel like freedom. It feels like a death.

Dear Diary,

"Is this what being in love feels like?" I asked you a few weeks ago while sitting in the front seat of your car. I was looking at you in adoration, like a little girl. Squinting my eyes from the sun streaming through the windshield. I will never forget the way you looked at me, with tears in your eyes. You told me you'd never really been in love before me. That nothing had ever felt like this until now.

My friends are sending me texts that feel like condolences. Like someone died.

I have this thing where I see the most beautiful parts of people. It's like a piece of my brain refuses to register the harm they cause. It's like I can overlook the bad things they do. The shitty choices they make. My therapist says it's a trauma thing. I'm sure he's right. I'm so sick of trauma things. I'm so sick of fucking up my eyelashes from crying. I'm so sick of remembering how safe I felt with you.

I defended who you are. I over-explained you. I took the blows for you. Tried to fix it. Tried to imagine it wasn't true. This can't happen, I kept telling myself. It can't fall apart like this. I waited so long for him. I wish I could hate you. I wish I could trust you. I wish you could have been the man I thought you were.

I was willing to change my whole life for you.

I read something on Instagram today that said: "What was the most pain you have ever felt?" Healing from someone I once thought I would heal with.

CHAPTER THIRTEEN

A CHANGE OF HEART

I didn't text Jackson because I missed my Chloe sunglasses. I texted him because I missed *him*.

He replied within seconds.

○ **Him:** Of course. I'll mail them to you today.

○ **Me:** Thank you.

○ **Him:** Anything. Always. Forever.

○ **Me:** I wish I could believe that.

○ **Him:** I do too. All I've ever wanted is to give you everything. I know you said you wanted space, but if you ever want to talk, I will stop my whole life for you.

Fuck.

I had been clean from Jackson for five weeks. Five weeks of silence. Five weeks of teaching myself not to reach for my phone, of going to bed without our goodnight phone calls, of forcing myself to eat when my stomach felt like it had caved in.

Five weeks of therapy, of dinner plans with friends, of

trying—*really* trying—to believe that moving forward was the right thing. And then, on a random Tuesday morning in June, something inside of me cracked.

I paced my apartment, my third coffee of the day cooling in my hands, rereading his message over and over. I could literally feel him pulling me in as my fingers hovered over my phone, my brain screaming *don't do it,* but my loneliness was louder. Before I could stop myself, I responded again. And just like that, the floodgates opened.

We talked all day. He told me how much he missed me, how sick he was of his own selfishness. How when he was with me, he was the man he'd always wanted to be.

I told him I was scared, that I didn't know if I could ever trust him again. That even now, part of me wanted to run, and part of me wanted to believe him. He told me he would call me, said he'd answer everything, that he'd give me the full truth, even the parts I wasn't ready for. He told me he was terrified, but he was willing.

That evening, my phone rang. It was the first time I had heard his voice in over a month. And the second I did, I felt the release. It felt like I had been holding my breath without realizing it, like my entire body had been clenched, waiting. It felt good. *Too* good.

I wanted to tell him everything. That my book had just been picked up in France. That I was planning a signing in Paris. That my nephew had started talking and said "boobies" instead of "movies" and it was the most adorable thing I'd ever heard. That I had been trying to keep myself busy, to do things that made me happy, but I felt *nothing*. And I hated that he was still the only one who made me feel *everything*.

Something so strange happens when you break up with your best friend. One day, they know every single thing about you—your thoughts before you even say them, the way you take your coffee, the stupid inside jokes no one else would understand. And then suddenly, they're just... gone. Living their life parallel to yours, existing in a world that no longer has you in it.

But that night, for the first time in five weeks, I let him back in.

And just like that, we were *us* again.

But just as quickly as I remembered how good it felt to talk to him, the echoes of those other women filled my mind. The rage was simmering beneath the surface. I had questions. I wanted to tell him everything they told me. And I needed to know if there was more.

He sat quietly on the other end of the line as I recounted every story. He took ownership of what was true. He admitted to things he had denied before. He apologized, again and again. Told me he wasn't that person anymore. And maybe I believed him before I should have.

He asked me how soon he could fly up to New York to see me. I told him to wait. Not until after Paris. I couldn't afford the distraction. If things went horribly wrong, I didn't want to carry that into this trip—this moment that was supposed to be *mine*.

♡

Paris was dreamy, but I was distracted. He checked in daily, from the other side of the world, cheering me on like he always had. I sent him updates and photos. He told me how proud he was. Every night, our goodnight calls stretched across time zones, his voice filling the space between my hotel room and the streets of a city that was supposed to feel like magic. I was supposed to be celebrating. I was supposed to be *free*. And yet, there he was. Still in my head. Still in my heart.

I landed back in New York feeling restless. I felt like I should have felt better. Paris had been a dream. My book signing was a huge success. I should've been floating. But instead, I was stuck in my head, already counting down the days until Jackson's flight.

A week later, he was here. Standing in front of me, in my doorway, looking at me like I was the only person on earth.

And yet, the second I saw him, something felt...off.

I had been waiting for this moment, replaying it in my mind over and over, convincing myself that seeing him would bring back the magic. That time apart would have changed something, cleared the air. Made us feel like *us* again.

But the truth settled into my bones the moment he wrapped his arms around me. It wasn't the same. I couldn't un-know what I knew.

He had told me everything. He had owned up to all of it, answered every question. Promised he'd get himself into therapy to work on things. Delicately and lovingly held my pain alongside his regret and remorse. There were no more secrets. No more hidden betrayals waiting to be uncovered. It was all in front of me. But for the first time since meeting him, none of it felt like relief.

It felt like a weight.

I couldn't see him the way I once had.

I wanted to. *God*, I wanted to. I wanted to lose myself in his arms again, soften into the rhythm of us, and let the past be the past. But something had shifted.

We tried to make it work for months. Back and forth from New York. Back and forth from hope to doubt. Some days, I swore we were stronger than ever. He was trying, really trying. The man who once avoided hard conversations now sat with me in them, unpacking his own flaws instead of excusing them. He was gentle with my triggers, patient with my pain, reminding me in a thousand little ways that he wasn't just here—he was choosing to be here.

He shared his location. Gave me the passcode to his phone. Gave me his word.

And as comforting as it all felt, the cracks in my mind remained.

There were days and weeks where we mapped out a future together that seemed almost possible. Then there were days and weeks where I lived in fear, wondering if I could go on with a man I still couldn't fully surrender to.

Because as much as I loved him, as much as I wanted to believe love could be enough, the trust never fully returned. The past lived with us like a stubborn ghost who wouldn't leave. Haunting me unexpectedly in the moments where I finally let my guard down. Interrupting my peace before I could ever rest in it.

I started picking fights over the smallest things. Tiny, insignificant things like text messages that weren't answered fast enough, a change in his tone, how long he lingered on his phone. It wasn't really about any of it. It was about everything.

I hated that I was becoming someone who needed proof. Proof that he wasn't lying. Proof that he wasn't slipping back into old patterns. Proof that I wasn't making another mistake.

I wanted so badly to believe him. But I had spent so much time wrestling with whether or not I could that I was losing myself in the process.

And if I had lost myself, how could I stay?

We spent months trying to outrun the inevitable. Because leaving someone you still love is one of the hardest things in the world. It's easier to stay and pretend. It's easier to stretch out the goodbye so it doesn't feel as brutal, as final. It's easier to convince yourself that if you just wait a little longer, love will find a way to rewrite the ending.

But deep down, I knew. I think he did too.

Dear Diary,

California is on fire and I still can't hit 130 grams of protein a day and I still hope every time my phone dings it's you.

And it never is because I told you I deserved more and you listened. So I fill my apartment with plants when I really want a cat instead or maybe a dog but I know that's a terrible idea.

I still check your location I still check the weather in your city I still wonder if I made a mistake.

I have a nightmare where I am alone at a beach waiting on a friend and she tells me she's running forty minutes late so I drink a warm can of wine and fall asleep. When I wake up everything I own is gone and my skin is burned red because I forgot sunscreen. I am angry at myself and I am crying. I knew I shouldn't have closed my eyes. I wake up with wet cheeks.

Grieving someone who is still very much alive is a version of hell one never gets used to. Grieving the fantasy of who you thought they were is worse.

I load my Delta app and furiously check flights to London. Maybe I can go next week for a few days. Just to get out of here. Just to reset.

I look back at our emails. Maybe he did change. Maybe I can deal with it. Maybe I can love him harder.

I walk to the kitchen and open a bottle of white wine. I crack the window. I feel a cold breeze whip my face and I tell myself that maybe . . .

I can finally stay still.

CHAPTER THIRTEEN

THE LAST GOODBYE?

I didn't leave Jackson just once—I left him over and over, for a whole year, each time believing it was the last, until leaving became the only way to find myself.

Like many love stories, ours wasn't a clean break. There was no single moment where everything shattered in a way that couldn't be repaired. Instead, there were cracks. Spreading, deepening, filling with apologies and promises, patched together with hope. Every time I walked away, I told myself I was done. And every time I went back, I told myself it would be different.

I stayed because I had invested more time. Because I had grown closer to his girls. Because I had built something in my mind that was too beautiful to burn down. But with every return, I uncovered something new. Another lie, another omission, another reason to go. The damage wasn't just lingering; it was multiplying.

I left him so many times that leaving became a ritual.

But through it all, he *tried*.

And maybe that's what made it hurt the most.

Jackson didn't fight to keep me out of selfishness—he fought because he *believed* in us. He wanted to be the man I saw in him. He wanted to change. He wanted to be better, for me, for himself, for his daughters. And for a long time, I wanted to believe that love could be enough to fix what was broken.

I wanted to believe *he* could be enough.

I wanted to believe *I* could be enough.

But love alone is not a foundation. It cannot replace trust. It cannot undo the past. And wanting to change is not the same as changing.

I was always searching for a sign. The final straw, the unbearable hurt, the undeniable proof that would make it impossible to turn back. But the truth is, I lost our relationship the moment I opened that first email. The moment I felt my body go cold, my stomach drop, my mind race to bargain with what I already knew. The moment I realized the man I loved was a man I did not know at all.

I think I represented something to Jackson—something intoxicating, something he craved but wasn't built to hold. A love that was endless and unconditional. Passionate and all-consuming. But *wanting* love and *being ready* for it are two different things, and no amount of coming back, no amount of patience, no amount of believing in him could make him become the man he wasn't ready to be.

And I was done waiting for him to catch up.

That didn't mean I didn't still hold a piece of hope in my heart for him.

Not hope that we'd find our way back to each other. Not hope that he'd magically transform overnight. But hope that someday, somehow, he *would* become the man he always wanted to be. That he *would* heal the parts of himself that pulled us apart. That he would learn how to love in the way he always swore he wanted to. The way he loved me, but without the fear, without the sabotage, without the weight of his past pulling him under. That he would learn how to love without the quiet ache of knowing he's falling short.

And maybe, in some distant, unknown future, our paths would cross again.

Maybe we'd be different people by then. Maybe we'd be strangers again, meeting for the first time.

Or maybe we wouldn't. Maybe we were only ever meant to be a lesson to each other. Maybe the *real* love story was the one I found in myself.

When I reached my end, I knew I had two choices: I could continue trying to save Jackson, or I could finally, fully, irrevocably save myself.

I chose myself.

Not because I stopped loving him. Not because I woke

up one morning and the ache had disappeared. But because, somewhere between the longing and the wreckage it left behind, I realized that every ounce of pain, every disappointment, every slow unraveling of the illusion wasn't just breaking me—it was bringing me back to myself.

Every argument, every doubt, every warning sign was a love letter written to myself in hot pink neon, glowing so bright it was impossible to ignore: *You deserve more. You deserve more. You deserve more.*

And I never stopped fighting for myself.

But it wasn't just Jackson who taught me that. It was Julian. It was Rick. It was Matteo. It was Alex. It was every ghost of my past who began as a love story and ended as a lesson. It was every night I spent alone, staring into the mirror, searching my own eyes for the answer that had been there all along. Because when everything else faded—when the texts stopped, when the flights were canceled, when the dream of what could have been finally died—I was the one who remained.

That's the thing about love. We spend our whole lives searching for it outside ourselves, chasing the high of someone choosing us, as if that choice is what makes us real. But when push comes to shove, when everything falls apart, the love we crave was never in their hands. It was in us all along.

I'll never regret the way I show up for love. I'll never regret wearing my heart on my sleeve, even when it leaves me bruised. I'll never regret fighting for something I believe in, even when it fails me. And I'll never regret risking it all for even just a taste of that impossible, fleeting, all-consuming thing we all chase.

Because at the end of the day, I know this much to be true: I don't need anyone else to write my love story. I am my *own* greatest love story. And I will never, ever leave myself behind.

♡

But closure is never as clean as we want it to be.

And love, no matter how far we run from it, always seems to find a way back to us. Some stories don't end when we think they do. Some have a way of continuing. Whether we're ready for them or not.

Time passed. I had done everything right. I walked away. I did the work. I played the part of a woman who had done the hard thing, who had chosen herself.

I went on dates, even when I didn't want to. I smiled at men across candlelit tables and tried to care about their stories, their lives. Tried to feel something—anything.

I went out with my friends. I let them hype me up, tell me how much better I was without him. I filled my days with work, travel, distractions. I convinced myself, over and over again, that I was doing the right thing. That the ache in my chest was just a withdrawal. That one day, it would fade.

But I couldn't unlearn what it felt like to love him.

I still reached for my phone at night, still heard him in every song lyric, still thought of him when something funny happened that only *we* would understand. I still checked the weather in his city. Still checked his location that he forgot to turn off.

I couldn't forget the way his voice softened when he called me *baby*, the slight drawl lingering long enough for me to bask in how desired I felt. The way he made me feel like I was *home* no matter where we were. The way we just knew each other, in ways I'd never known anyone before.

I couldn't forget that no matter how much I wanted to move on, no one else felt like him.

And I knew that no one else ever would.

But he still had work to do. He still had parts of himself to unravel, wounds to heal, things he needed to face. And I couldn't save him.

So I told myself I had to let go.

One night, I was lying in bed, trying to will myself to sleep, the glow of my phone screen the only light in the room.

And then, it happened.

The screen lit up with his name.

I started shaking. I held the phone in my hand, staring at it in shock.

Jackson calling…

It was 10:24 p.m.

I will always pick up the phone when you call, we'd tell each other, even in the worst times.

I could answer. I could let his voice wash over me like it

always had, let myself believe in him, in us, in whatever version of this story we were still writing.

Or I could let it ring. Let the moment pass. Stay strong. Let him become another name, another *what-if*, another story.

I stared at his name for another few seconds. It felt like an hour.

I clutched the phone in my hand, took a deep breath, and made my choice.

ACKNOWLEDGEMENTS

This book would not exist without the people who lived through it with me—sometimes against their will. To my ride-or-dies, the ones who got every chapter of this book in the form of long, dramatic voice notes and over wine-filled, tear-soaked dinners: Blaine, JoJamie, Nicole, Gwen, Tara, Brie, Odalys, Ashlina, Jacques, and Morgan. Thank you for letting me spiral, for always picking up the phone, and for never telling me to *just block him already* (even when I probably should have).

To my mom—my rock, my safe place, the woman who has heard it all (and I do mean *all*) and never once judged me. Your unwavering love is everything. To my brother, another rock in my life, thank you for always being in my corner.

To my readers—whether you've been with me for 17 years (almost 20, what?!) or just found your way into my world—you are the reason I keep telling stories. A special shoutout to my

Substack subscribers, especially the paid ones (*bless you*), who got sneak peeks of many of these chapters before they were released. Your support means the world to me.

To Chloe Caldwell, my writing mentor-turned-dear friend, who gave me the push I needed to make this book happen. Chloe, you are a gift.

To Zoe Norvell, who designed the gorgeous book you're holding in your hands—I'm obsessed.

To every stage that let me test-drive these dating disasters in front of an audience: *Generation Women, Love Notes, Miss Manhattan, Wine and Pine*—I appreciate you all. And the biggest love to Melissa Meier, who not only believed in my stories but gave me a stage of my very own so I could bring *The Tortured Bloggers Department* to life. Melissa, and the entire bar team that lets me hijack their space with a microphone and my unhinged tales—thank you for making my storytelling dreams come true.

This book is for every woman who has ever texted her ex when she *knew* she shouldn't. For every friend who has sat across from a heartbroken bestie, topping off her glass, nodding along, and saying, *"Babe… I hear you."*

And for every writer who has ever thought, *Can I really tell this story?*—yes, you can. And you absolutely should.

And lastly, to the men who made this book possible—whether you ghosted, love-bombed, breadcrumbed, or truly loved me—congratulations, you are now immortalized in print. Some of you were lessons, some of you were poetry, and all of you were necessary. Either way, you gave me a story to tell. No royalties will be issued. Wishing you all the best (but mostly therapy).

Cheers to love, heartbreak, and writing our way through it.

♡

ABOUT THE AUTHOR

CARA ALWILL is a bestselling author, writing and publishing mentor, and creator of *Cara Says It All*, dedicated to helping women own their voices and tell their stories with confidence. With over 300,000 books sold worldwide, her work has been translated into ten languages, including French, Ukrainian, Chinese, and Russian. From self-publishing to landing deals with major publishers like Penguin Random House, Cara's literary career is proof that women can build powerful writing empires on their own terms.

As the creator of *Hot Girl Memoir* and *Literary Queens: Own Your Voice, Craft Your Story, Create Your Publishing Empire on Substack and Beyond*, Cara teaches women how to craft compelling narratives and navigate the world of publishing with confidence. She also teaches writing courses for *Write or Die* magazine, furthering her mission to help women refine their craft and share their voices unapologetically.

In addition to her books and courses, Cara is the host of the *Cara Says It All* podcast and the founder of *The Tortured Bloggers Department*, a live NYC storytelling series that celebrates raw, real, and unfiltered writing. Whether she's mentoring aspiring authors, penning her next bestseller, or speaking on stage, Cara is committed to one thing: empowering women to write their own rules—and their own stories.

Connect with Cara on Instagram
@TheChampagneDiet

Learn more about Cara and her coaching
services at www.carasaysitall.com

---

www.ingramcontent.com/pod-product-compliance
Lightning Source LLC
LaVergne TN
LVHW041223080426
835508LV00011B/1051